# SHE AND HER CAT

# She and Her Cat

MAKOTO SHINKAI AND
NARUKI NAGAKAWA

Translated by Ginny Tapley Takemori

doubleday

TRANSWORLD PUBLISHERS
Penguin Random House, One Embassy Gardens,
8 Viaduct Gardens, London SW11 7BW
www.penguin.co.uk

Transworld is part of the Penguin Random House group of companies
whose addresses can be found at global.penguinrandomhouse.com

First published in Great Britain in 2022 by Doubleday
an imprint of Transworld Publishers.
First published in Japanese as *Kanojo To Kanojo No Neko* in 2013 by Kanzen Corp.

A CIP catalogue record for this book
is available from the British Library.

ISBN 9780857528223

Typeset in 10.5/14pt Dante MT Std by Jouve (UK), Milton Keynes
Printed and bound in Great Britain by Clays Ltd, Elcograf S.p.A.

The authorized representative in the EEA is Penguin Random House Ireland,
Morrison Chambers, 32 Nassau Street, Dublin D02 YH68.

Penguin Random House is committed to a sustainable future
for our business, our readers and our planet. This book is made
from Forest Stewardship Council® certified paper.

I

SEA OF WORDS

It was a wet day in early spring.

Dense, fog-like rain fell on me as I lay at the side of the road, my cheek plastered against the bottom of a cardboard box. Pedestrians gave me sideways glances as they rushed on past. Eventually, I could no longer lift my head, and was left gazing up at the leaden sky through one eye.

In the hushed surroundings, the sound of an approaching train boomed like distant thunder. It blared out regular and strong as it moved along the elevated tracks overhead and it aroused a strong yearning in me. If the faint heartbeat I could hear within my chest was enough to move me, how big a thing this sound must be able to move!

Surely it must be the sound of the world's heart. The strong, big, perfect world. A world I wasn't to be part of.

The fine rain fell continuously without making a sound. Lying there in the box, I had the illusion that I was slowly rising.

I was rising up and up high into the sky. Before long there would be a *snap* and I would be severed from this world.

My mother was the first to secure me to this life. She was warm and gentle and gave me everything I desired, but she was gone now.

I couldn't remember what had happened or why I was here in a cardboard box getting drenched in the rain.

We can't remember everything, only the parts that are truly important. But there wasn't a single thing I wanted to remember.

The soft rain kept falling.

The empty shell of myself rose slowly up into the grey sky. I closed my eyes, waiting.

The sound of the train seemed to be getting louder. I opened my eye to see a woman's face. She was holding a large plastic umbrella and peering down at me.

How long had she been there?

She squatted down and looked at me, resting her chin on her knees. A strand of hair hung over her forehead. The train seemed louder than ever, as if echoing under the umbrella.

Her hair and my fur were heavy from the rain, filling our surroundings with a lovely smell.

I carefully lifted my head and glanced directly up at her.

Her eyes wavered. She looked away for a moment, then turned back to me with determination, as if making up her mind. We gazed intently at each other like this for a while.

'Shall we go, then? Together.'

I felt her fingers, cold as ice, against my body as she scooped me up into her arms. I looked down at the cardboard box, surprised by how small it was. She tucked me between her jacket and sweater. Her body was incredibly warm, and I could hear her heartbeat.

As the roar of the train overtook us, she set off walking. The heartbeats of she, me and the world pulsed together as one.

That was the day she took me in. I was now her cat.

Society is mostly made up of words.

I began to realize this once I got a job and went out into the world. It was all 'Get this done!' or 'Tell so-and-so this!' Work progressed only through a vague exchange of words that immediately dissipated. Everyone got on with things as if this were completely normal, but to me it was almost miraculous.

I enjoyed dealing with documents. They felt permanent. My colleagues didn't seem to like this kind of work, so I readily took it upon myself to do it and was thus considered useful to my workmates.

Certainly, I felt more comfortable working with documents than with people. I was not a good communicator, and would find myself running out of things to say almost immediately. My friends loved to talk, though. Whenever I spent time with Tamaki, whom I'd known since our student days, witty remarks came effortlessly out of her, sending me into fits of laughter. Tamaki could draw meaning from any situation, as if she could see things that I didn't. I always found her astonishing.

I liked talkative people.

My boyfriend's name was Nobu. He was a year younger than me, and he talked A LOT. About his job at an insurance company, about sci-fi movies and electronic music. About ancient wars in China. He would share all sorts of things with me.

Thanks to him, I knew a lot about the insurance system, and about the names of warlords.

My friend Tamaki was good at putting external things into words, while Nobu was good at expressing what he'd stored inside. I couldn't do either.

The arrival of spring reminds me of the day I first rented my own apartment, especially on a rainy day like today.

I went around visiting estate agents, and nervously put my seal on a contract. I was to live on my own for the first time.

It was raining the day I moved in, too. Tamaki came over to help me, and brought her younger colleague Nobu along with her.

After unpacking and putting up some shelves, we went for a meal at a local eatery.

It was the first time a friend and some guy had ever helped me move, and it felt unreal, like something in a TV drama series, but I couldn't quite express this in words. Then Tamaki said, 'This reminds me of when we were students!' and Nobu laughed.

I tried to smile, but I realized that normal people did this kind of thing all the time.

Living alone would not change me after all.

Soon after I moved in to my apartment, Nobu came to visit.

There was a loose connection on my washing machine, and water often leaked from the hose. When I had complained about this to Tamaki, she'd arranged for Nobu to fix it.

I'd assumed Tamaki would come too, so I was a bit taken aback when he turned up alone. He'd bought a bunch of stuff at the DIY centre and fixed the leak for me. I didn't even know that I had to turn the water off at the mains.

How nice it would be to have a man around, I thought. I was surprised by how easily I managed to express this feeling to Nobu.

It was the first time I'd ever been able to communicate so directly.

He stayed with me that night. The idea that words could change my world was a little scary.

We began meeting at my place every week, until suddenly Nobu became very busy at work and I started to see less of him.

As far as I was concerned, he was my boyfriend and we understood each other, even if he didn't exactly put his feelings for me into words.

The stories in the girls' manga magazines we used to take turns reading at school always ended when the girl had got herself a boyfriend, but I discovered that's not what happens in real life.

Even when you have a boyfriend, there are times when you feel terribly lonely, more so than when you didn't have one.

Today, I met up with Nobu for the first time in three months. We walked side by side in the spring rain. Even after so long, he was affectionate, and talked as though nothing had changed.

Letting myself drift along with his chat felt good. But when he'd gone, I was overwhelmed with anxiety. Almost like swimming in the sea and suddenly realizing you can't touch the bottom with your feet.

'We *are* going out together, aren't we?'

I just could never bring myself to come out with these words. If he said we should split up, I would definitely sink.

Today, too, I skirted around what I really wanted to say, instead orbiting him like a satellite round the Earth.

I was just like a little school kid. It was probably because I hadn't dealt properly with this sort of experience when I was still at school that these things were happening to me now.

In the end, he never did say the one thing I wanted to hear.

We said goodbye near his office. It would probably be a long time before we saw each other again, I thought.

When I got to my station, I took a different route home

than usual. It was a long way round, but I felt like walking in the cold rain.

And that's when I came across the cat.

Her apartment smelled so comfortingly of her. The first morning I spent there, I was surprised by how warm it was. I'd never woken up in such a warm space before.

She was already up, and was busy heating water on the stove.

'Good morning!' she said, as I watched the steam gush from the spout of the kettle.

Then she flung open the curtains. The clouds were tinted by a beautiful sunrise.

Her apartment was on the first floor of a block of flats at the top of a slope. You could see the train going over the raised tracks from there.

That's when I discovered it was this train that had been making the sound which had so impressed me before. I was so excited by this discovery that I told her about it.

'Sure, Chobi, that's great!'

Chobi?

'Chobi. That's your name.'

That was the first time she called me by a name. Chobi. I liked it, this name she'd given me.

I would remember this morning for ever, I thought.

★

I fell in love with her instantly.

She was beautiful, and kind. Whenever she caught me looking at her, her face would soften and she'd smile gently.

She prepared my food before eating her own: a dish of milk, some tinned meat and some crunchy dry biscuits.

While I lapped up my milk, she'd crouch down next to me cradling a large mug of warm milk in her hands. We each drank side by side like this.

Her movements were relaxed and graceful, and I felt calm around her.

I'd eat half the food she put out for me, instinct telling me I should leave some for later in case anything happened, and then flop down at her side, rolling over to show her my tummy. She would slowly circle her hand on my belly while I swayed my tail in satisfaction.

I liked to climb on to her tummy, too, whenever she lay down on the floor. She would usually be reading, and would stroke my back in silence.

I liked to watch her do the laundry. The clothes still smelled of her, and I snuggled my whole body into them ecstatically.

I liked to watch her hang the laundry out to dry as well. We'd wander out on to the balcony together, and I'd gaze contentedly at the blue sky, the cars and the passers-by below.

I slept on one of her sweaters, which she'd placed in a bed for me. It was the white one she'd been wearing the first time I met her.

In the early days, I'd often wake up mewling in the

middle of the night from a bad dream. She would always stay beside me, gently stroking my fur.

She cooked her own meals, and I especially liked to watch her make miso soup because she always gave me bits of dried fish. I really liked it when she ate cold tofu, too, because she would sprinkle dried bonito flakes on to my food.

She used to sing to herself while cooking, and I loved hearing her sing.

'Chobi.'

She always called me this. Through this name I connected to her, and through her to the world.

I woke up every morning at the same time, prepared breakfast, watched the same TV programme, and left for work, always in that order.

Since I'd started living on my own, I'd found joy in creating an orderly lifestyle. It was comforting to discover that I could control my routine.

Even when Chobi came to live with me, my life didn't change much. I'd had a dog growing up and it had been a hassle having to take him out for a walk even when it was pouring with rain or snowing, but cats are creatures that don't need much looking after.

Today, as always, I woke up a moment before the alarm sounded and turned it off. I could feel Chobi's presence in my room. I took the thermometer from under my pillow and measured my basal body temperature. I'd been keeping a daily chart since I'd started going out with Nobu. Now that it had become a habit, it would have felt weird to stop, and all the records I'd kept until now would have been a waste of time.

Bathed in the morning sun streaming through the window, I made my breakfast of small rice balls. Any that I didn't eat would go in my lunch bento.

Chobi and I drank our milk, then I changed into my work clothes. I almost forgot the time as I watched Chobi wrestling with my pyjamas.

I liked watching her reflection as she stood in front of the mirror, putting on her make-up. With practised movements she spread out an array of brushes, using each one in turn, before carefully putting them all away again. She did everything meticulously.

Lastly, she applied her perfume. Its fragrance spread through the apartment, smelling of grass wet from the rain.

As always, she watched the TV weather forecast for the day. Then it was time for her to leave.

I really loved watching her tie up her long black hair, put on a jacket in matching black, and slip her feet into high-heeled shoes.

She crouched down to where I was sitting by the front

door and gave my head a gentle stroke with the tips of her fingers.

'See you later, Chobi,' she said, then she stood up with her back absolutely straight and pulled open the heavy metal door.

I narrowed my eyes against the sunshine that streamed across the threshold.

See you later!

She stepped out into the light.

Feeling the lingering presence of her fingers on my head, I listened to the sound of her heels clacking pleasantly as she made her way down the outside staircase and into the distance.

After seeing her off, I climbed up on to a chair and watched as a train travelled over the raised tracks beyond the balcony. Maybe she was on it.

I watched the trains till I'd had my fill, then jumped back down off the chair.

The smell of her perfume still hung in the air. Enveloped in the fragrance, I went back to sleep.

Swaying inside the packed train, I thought of Chobi.

Whenever he was asleep or absorbed in something, however much I called his name, he pretended not to hear, but he would roll over and show his tummy when he wanted attention.

If I stepped over him pretending not to notice, he'd dash off then roll over in front of me, flashing his tummy again. It was so unbearably cute.

I felt myself smiling suddenly and quickly composed my face. Some colleagues and students used this train, and I'd be embarrassed to be caught with a dumb expression.

It was so nice to have someone waiting for me at home. I caught sight of an ad above the train door for a matchmaking service. Maybe this was what people meant by marital bliss. The joy of my cat.

A friend my age was already married. She'd scored early, marrying her boyfriend from college on graduation. On the New Year's card she'd sent to my parents' place, there was a photo of her holding a small baby with her husband at her side. I tried to imagine Nobu and me in their place, but it didn't feel very real and I smiled wryly.

I couldn't even ask him if we were actually going out together. If I got pregnant, would he even marry me?

And in any case, did I really want to get married?

I imagined myself growing old, living in my little apartment, surrounded by lots of cats.

I heard the announcement that the train was approaching my stop.

I stood up as straight as I could and got off the train.

In my job as an administrator at a technical college for art and design, there were always a lot of bulky documents to manage. This morning when I arrived, some had spilled over from my colleague's desk and knocked over my pen-holder, but pointing it out seemed a bit petty. The desks shouldn't be this small in the first place, I told myself, as I turned on my computer.

I woke up from my nap and had a big long stretch before deciding to go out for a walk. I could get out on to the balcony through a hole in the kitchen wall that had been made for a vent when the gas stove or something was installed. She'd turned it into a door for me after realizing I wanted to go outside.

'You might not be able to get through it when you grow bigger, though. We'll have to come up with something else by then,' she said. But we cats could get through much smaller spaces than she thought, so it was fine, at least for now.

The weather today was clear with a fresh breeze. I squeezed my head through a gap in the balcony railings to watch the train, the flow of cars, and people on the street below. Having ascertained that the world was in motion, I leaped on to the next balcony and then to the one after that to reach finally the external staircase.

There was an abundance of smells outside. The smell of the earth and other animals carried on the breeze, the smell coming from some kitchen or other, of exhaust fumes and the garbage collection point.

Once I'd landed on the ground, I lifted my head up

towards her apartment. The building was a two-storey affair sandwiched between two other tall ones. All the windows were the same, but somehow her apartment looked special.

I roamed around the block. We cats had territories, and the area around her apartment building was mine. I sniffed here and there, checking whether other cats had been over or not, then left my mark.

To be honest, I wasn't all that bothered about who owned which territory, but it was a cat's instinct, so I couldn't help it.

And so my regular patrol was done. But now that I'd grown used to the area, it occurred to me to maybe broaden my horizons a little.

I headed for the top of the slope on the opposite side of the raised tracks. No other cat smells had wafted over from there.

It was best to have a large territory. That was our instinct. But it was also a bother having to deal with trouble from other cats.

I made my way along the tops of fences and under the cover of plants, to avoid being run over or disturbed by anyone.

Eventually, I reached a house with a garden full of greenery.

I could tell right away why there weren't any other cats living around here. At the bottom of the garden was a big dog. It looked old, with floppy ears and black and white patches on its fur.

Dogs never welcomed cats and I was just about to take my leave, when, of all things, it called out to me.

'It's been a long time, Shiro.'

The dog sounded so remarkably easy-going that I did a double-take. It didn't seem to be putting on any airs at all, despite its size.

'Er, hello,' I answered.

'As beautiful as ever, I see!'

Beautiful? This dog obviously couldn't tell the difference between male and female cats.

'Er, but I'm male,' I said, a little irritated. After checking it was on a chain, naturally.

'Is that so?' It didn't seem annoyed in the slightest and added, 'Well, in that case, a splendid male.'

'Thank you,' I answered graciously. What a peculiar dog. My curiosity was aroused. 'My name is Chobi, not Shiro.'

The dog looked at me, its eyes wide with surprise.

'Chobi, is it? Not Shiro? My mistake, sorry. You're both white cats. This was Shiro's territory.'

I was disappointed to hear another cat had got here before me.

'But there aren't any other cats here. I can't smell any.'

'That's right. I'm guarding the place for Shiro, so they don't come close.'

This dog said the oddest things.

'I've never heard of a dog guarding a cat's territory before.'

'I promised Shiro I would.'

'Well, where did this Shiro go?'

'I haven't seen her for a while now. The last time I saw her she had a large belly.'

Oh! Even I couldn't miss the implication of this. A cat identical to me, a pure white cat . . .

'In that case, she must be my mother,' I managed to say. The reason I was all alone and the area at the top of the slope didn't smell of cat was one and the same: Shiro was no longer alive.

The dog took a deep breath.

'Jon,' he said.

'Jon?'

'That's my name. I'm now going to tell you something very important. I think it's best you know.'

'Understood, Jon.'

'Chobi, did Shiro treat you affectionately?'

'I don't remember, but I'd like to think she did.'

'I see . . .' Jon didn't say anything for a while, then suddenly changed the subject. 'Shiro and I were like sweethearts.'

'Sweethearts?'

'All beautiful women are my sweethearts, you know!'

'Ah.'

'Shiro had the same lovely white fur as you,' Jon said dreamily.

'Thank you.'

My fur was lovely because *she* always brushed me.

'I've often wondered about you and your siblings.'

Hearing this, my chest constricted a little.

'From now on, Chobi, this will be your territory.'

'Really? Are you sure?'

'Shiro would certainly approve. And it will be proof that she lived here, too.'

'Thank you, Jon!'

'All for the sake of a beautiful sweetheart, you know.' He gave a big yawn. 'Come and see me again whenever you like.'

With the conversation apparently over, he went back to sleep, using his front paws as a pillow for his big round head.

I trotted back down the slope, thinking how strange it all was.

I'd been close to being severed from the world when *she* had saved me, and I'd somehow managed to survive. Then, I went out walking on a whim and happened to meet Jon, who told me about my mother and allowed me to inherit her territory.

I'd almost been cut loose, but now I felt myself engaging once more.

I was back in the world.

Lunch break. I ate my bento at my desk, then walked round to a small cafe near my office. It was a little pricey, but students never came in so I could relax.

I ordered a coffee, then realized I hadn't told Nobu about Chobi yet. I hardly ever called him these days. He was always so busy, but that wasn't the only reason. I was scared. If I couldn't keep the conversation going, I might say something that would put him off me.

But Chobi was something I could talk about.

Did Nobu actually like cats? Maybe he hated them. I

didn't even know. He'd told me lots of things, but that was one thing he'd never mentioned.

I looked up his number in my call history and pressed dial. The date of the last call was quite a long time ago. In the early days, we'd spoken all the time.

It kept ringing and then switched to voicemail. *I can't answer the phone right now. Please leave a message.*

I felt suddenly deflated, and hung up without saying anything. I sighed and sank back in the cafe armchair.

My phone vibrated. I looked hurriedly at the screen: a message from Tamaki. *I'll come see you in Golden Week!* she wrote excitedly, peppering it with emojis.

It was just like her to be pushy. *Looking forward to it!* I replied. That didn't seem quite enough, so I sent a photo of Chobi, too.

The waiter brought my coffee. I took a sip, then decided to text Nobu. He hardly ever texted. He was the type who wanted to chat if he had something to say.

*I've adopted a cat. He's called Chobi.*

I thought for some time – the text looked pretty uninspiring, so I attached a photo of Chobi. I considered sending a picture of myself, too, but then decided against it.

All the pictures I had of Chobi were of him showing his tummy.

She always came home at the same time.

Hearing her heels clacking up the concrete stairs outside,

I ran to the front door to wait for her. Finally, the heavy door opened and she appeared.

'Welcome back,' I said.

'Hi, Chobi!'

She gave my head a little stroke, and kicked off her shoes. She would often even pick me up for a cuddle.

Arriving home, she would always bring so many outside smells with her. The smell of other people, of soil from a place I'd never been to. A smell I didn't recognize. I savoured them all, and rubbed the back of my head on her ankles to top up my own scent that had begun to grow weak on her.

There was a lot to tell her about today. About meeting Jon, about visiting my mother's territory, about the new smells she'd brought home.

She stood in the kitchen listening to me while she opened a can of food for my dinner.

I was still babbling on about my mother when her phone rang.

It was probably Nobu.

I turned off the heat, put down the cooking chopsticks, and reached for my phone. Unfortunately, it was my mother's name on the screen.

'Hello.'

Chobi was making a racket, sharpening his claws on the

cardboard scratcher. He looked upset, so maybe he'd been taken aback by the phone ringing.

'Oh my, Miyu. You do sound a bit down.'

My mother had picked up on my despondency that it wasn't Nobu calling.

'Not particularly.'

'I suppose you thought it was your boyfriend, so you're disappointed it's only your mother.'

I didn't know how to respond to that fastball, so I said nothing.

'So, have you already got yourself a boyfriend? Introduce him to me, won't you? Is he nice?'

'No, no, it's nothing like that.'

'Oh well. Anyway, what are your plans for Golden Week?'

'A friend's coming over. Sorry.'

'Your boyfriend?'

'I said a friend. Tamaki, from my college days.'

'Oh, Tama-chan. Ha ha ha! I don't mind so much, but your dad seems to miss you. Do come and show your face from time to time.'

'Okay.'

'Have you got enough rice?'

'Loads.'

'Are you sure? I've just sent you some more.'

I wished she'd asked me before sending it.

'Is there anything you want?'

'Not particularly.'

'Oh. Well, take care, then.'

She hung up. She was always the same, never listening

to what anyone said. How weird that she'd given birth to someone like me. Even so, I felt a little better after speaking to her. It was like she'd shared some of her energy with me.

I used that energy to send Nobu a text.

*What are you doing for Golden Week?*

His reply came as I was boiling some udon noodles.

*Working, sorry.*

Just two words. No response to the photo of Chobi.

I sighed.

I ended up overcooking the noodles, what with turning the heat on and off to check my messages. I sprinkled half a pack of dried bonito flakes over them and emptied the rest on to the canned meat in Chobi's dish.

Chobi was super-excited by the smell. He was getting a big treat today.

I was sorting through the photos on my phone when I came across a picture of Nobu and me together. We were with the mascot at the most famous theme park in Japan.

Just looking at it made me feel depressed.

Chobi clambered on to my lap and poked his head up over the edge of the table.

'This is me,' I told him, showing him the photo. I looked somewhat uncomfortable in it, I thought. 'And this is my boyfriend.'

Chobi gazed curiously at the photo.

I woke up in time for my nightly patrol. She was still awake and typing something on her phone by the light of a small lamp. It was unusual for her to stay up so late. She'd changed into her pyjamas, so she must have already had her bath.

I padded quietly around the apartment, trying not to disturb her. I checked that nothing was out of place, drank a little of the water in my bowl, polished off the remains of my dinner, then jumped up on to her lap.

'No, I'd better not,' she muttered, then deleted everything she'd typed on her phone.

I saw she had the same expression as the one in the photo she'd shown me at dinnertime. A kind of frozen smile on her face.

I'd like to learn how to read too, I thought, as I got into my bed where she'd spread out her sweater for me, and fell asleep.

Tamaki came over in Golden Week.

She had talked of us going away somewhere, but I'd told her I now had a cat, so she came over to my apartment instead.

I cooked a meal, and we drank beer and chatted about nothing in particular while watching a DVD she'd brought with her.

Chobi immediately took to her and let her stroke his tummy.

'He's so fickle!' she said, and laughed.

'Friends are the best,' I said.

'Men!' Tamaki said, suddenly sulky. Apparently, some guy she was interested in was quite insensitive and hadn't noticed how she felt about him.

Come to think of it, I hadn't told her about Nobu yet. I'd planned on telling her when we were formally an item, but that hadn't happened yet and I kept letting it slide . . . In the end, I hadn't been able to come out with it.

Tamaki only stayed a day, but I laughed more than I had all month. Thanks to her, I'd dispelled the fog in my mind and felt more full of energy than I had for ages.

One of the students at the college where I worked was extraordinarily good at painting.

According to our most experienced teacher, Kamata-sensei, there were only one or two really talented students in each year. This one was called Reina, and she was gifted at painting natural objects in unusual colours. I always looked forward to seeing her assignments.

But she never got good comments on her work from the teacher or the other students, since she behaved so badly in class.

'Hey, Miyu, have you got a boyfriend?' she asked me. As if we were friends! A colleague said it was a sign she wanted to get closer to me.

'No comment.' I was used to this job and never got flustered.

'I think Masato likes you. His last work was the spitting image of you.'

Masato was a boy in her class. She was still quite childish in some ways, I thought.

'Anyway, how about handing in your assignment?'

'Okaaay.'

She showed me a rough sketch, which was as brilliant as ever.

After she'd gone back to her classroom, I sneaked a look at Masato's work. It looked more like Reina than me, I thought.

Kamata-sensei picked up Reina's sketch. 'It's not so much a matter of developing talent as not losing it. Like Kenji Miyazawa's poem says: all the talent and power and resources people may possess will not remain with them for ever.'

His eyes took on a faraway look, then he added, 'People, too, will some day cease to be themselves . . . That's how it goes.'

That sounded awfully heavy to me.

Summer came, and I found myself a friend.

I first set eyes on Mimi while out for a walk patrolling my territory. She was still just a kitten. I rarely came across cats smaller than me and I couldn't bring myself to chase her away, so I decided to leave her be. She'd probably wander off somewhere before long.

The next day, Mimi started to follow me on my rounds. As I threaded my way from one patch of shade to the next to avoid the harsh summer sun, before I knew it, she was following close on my heels.

I didn't say anything. I didn't want to get involved.

As I approached Jon's house, the cicadas in the trees all started chirring at once, and I flinched.

'Hey, know what that sound is?' Mimi asked.

'Just bugs,' I told her.

'Wrong!' she said gleefully.

'Well, what, then?'

'It's calling the rain,' she said, as if confiding a secret.

'No way.'

'Wanna test it?'

We sat together waiting for it to rain.

Eventually, it really did start raining.

'I won! You have to listen to me now.'

'I don't remember talking about winning or losing.'

'Anyway, I won. So play again with me tomorrow, okay?'

She rubbed her flank against mine. I jumped away like a shot.

'Okay, okay!'

'Don't forget!'

So the next day I went for a walk with Mimi, and again the cicadas chirred and it rained. No big deal. Evening showers are normal in summer.

The day after that, too, Mimi was waiting for me when I went out for my walk. She was really good at getting her way

One day she took me to an old wooden apartment building. I felt nervous passing right by another cat's territory, but Mimi didn't seem bothered at all.

A rickety shutter suddenly opened, and a young woman poked her head out. She had short hair and wasn't wearing any make-up. Not my type at all.

'Here again, are you?' the woman said. Her head disappeared, and soon after she wandered over to us.

I panicked and crawled under a nearby car, but Mimi kept her cool. 'Let me introduce her. This is Reina.'

Reina told us to wait a moment and went back inside to fetch something. She came out again carrying a dish with canned food in it, but it smelled completely different from the food I usually ate.

'Here you go,' she said. 'Enjoy!'

Mimi allowed me to share some, and I tried it cautiously. It was the first time I'd eaten anything that *she* hadn't given to me. It was an oily kind of fish I'd never tasted before.

On the way home, we saw a bird building a nest in a large pylon.

'Catch it for me!' Mimi demanded, staring fixedly at the bird.

'What do you want it for?'

'I said I want it.' She waved her long tail, determined.

'It's too high up for me.'

'Spoilsport!'

She was just a kid. I therefore decided to ignore her provocation.

'Whatever,' she said, and stalked off.

Anyway, I prefer mature women.

\*

Another day, out for a walk, I was sitting on some cool shaded concrete, enjoying the breeze, when Mimi came and coiled herself around me. She always did that without bothering to ask whether she was welcome or not.

'Hey, Chobi!'

'What?'

She climbed on top of me and I rolled over.

'Let's get married!'

'Look, Mimi, I've told you time and time again, I have a grown-up girlfriend,' I said, picturing *her* in my mind.

'Liar.'

'It's true,' I said, though she had me pinned under her.

'Introduce me to her!'

'No.' I'm *her* cat.

'Why not?'

'Mimi, how many times have I told you? You shouldn't be talking about this sort of thing until you're a bit older.' She was still just a kitten, after all.

'Spoilsport.' She waved her tail irritably.

'You have an owner too, don't you, Mimi? It's that sort of feeling.'

'Reina's not my owner. She just gives me food.'

'So what's your relationship with her like?'

'I don't know.'

We carried on chatting about nothing special for a while.

Beyond the clear blue sky, a gigantic white column of clouds was beginning to form.

Today, too, the cicadas were at full volume. Mimi

dampened her front paw and rubbed her face. By this time, we could instinctively tell when rain was approaching.

'Better get home before it starts raining.'

'Come play with me again, okay?' Mimi said. She looked terribly lonely.

'I will.'

'Definitely come again. Really. Really really really come, okay?'

This exchange repeated endlessly, so it had already started to rain by the time I was on my way home.

Mimi sweetly saw me off, then vanished in an instant. Maybe she'd gone back to that wooden apartment building.

The big wide sky was now covered with low dark clouds.

As I ran in the rain, it occurred to me that it would be good if *she* were as successful as Mimi at wheedling to get her own way.

I lost my best friend during the summer break.

There had been signs of it, I thought. It happened because I'd stifled my fears and hadn't said what I should have said. I only had myself to blame.

I'd just been too scared to admit it.

That day, Chobi had been acting a bit strangely too, pacing aimlessly around the apartment. Maybe he'd picked up on my feelings.

Tamaki had come over as arranged, and we'd been chatting away about nothing in particular, as usual. Then, after a pause, Tamaki suddenly said, 'You know, I really liked him.'

I gulped. I should have asked about her feelings from the beginning.

'You must have realized that. There's no way you couldn't have known.'

Tamaki had never said anything about fancying Nobu. How was I supposed to know if she didn't tell me? But, at the same time, I also thought it was partly my fault for not picking up on how she felt.

It was the same old problem: I just didn't pick up on things that normal people understood. I didn't understand the meaning behind the sea of words; I just kept drifting on the surface.

If I'd known how Tamaki had felt about Nobu, this would never have happened. I wanted to tell her this, but somehow couldn't find the words. All I said was, 'Things aren't going very well between Nobu and me any more.'

She glared at me. I'd never seen her look so scary.

When I didn't say anything, Chobi flipped over on to his front and looked up at me anxiously. He grazed my arm with his paw, his pads cool on my skin.

Tamaki gathered up everything she'd ever lent me and left. Among the things she took with her was a large food processor I'd never used, not even once. She'd brought it over saying she'd won it in a game of bingo at the after-party of a friend's wedding.

I've just lost my best friend, I thought, as I watched her leave.

I kept calling Nobu every day, and three days later he finally answered.

'Are we going out together?' I managed to ask him. My voice came out hoarse because I was nervous, but I was able to put into words what I'd wanted to ask for ages. Even that had taken so long.

'Aren't we?' he asked back.

How devious he is, I thought for the first time. 'I don't want to go out with you any more,' I told him.

'Have you got another boyfriend?'

'That's not the reason.'

'Well, if that's the case . . .' he said, and started chatting away in his usual calm and gentle tone. By now, everything he said sounded so frivolous, and I couldn't trust him. There wasn't even anything particularly great about his sea of words, which had seemed so rich to me before.

'I don't want to hear any of this,' I said without thinking, and realized it was true. Then the words poured out, one after another, as if filling in all the gaps that had been there until now.

To be honest, I probably had realized Tamaki had feelings for him, but had convinced myself otherwise. That's why I hadn't been able to secure my situation with Nobu – whether we really were an item or not. If that had been settled, I'd have been betraying Tamaki.

It hurt. But I realized our relationship had probably been quite a comfortable arrangement for Nobu.

'I never knew you could talk so much.'

That was the last thing he said to me.

And that's how I lost both my best friend and my boyfriend.

It was the middle of the night, and the rain was beating down on the concrete balcony.

After talking for ages on the phone, she'd started crying. I didn't know why. I'd never seen her like this before. But she sat for a long time with her head buried in her knees, weeping.

I didn't think she'd done anything wrong. I was the only one who saw her every day. She was always so much kinder and lovelier than anyone else, trying harder than anyone to live her best life.

'Hey, Chobi,' she said through her tears.

Her chair had tipped over and she was huddled beside it. A steady tone came from her phone, still clutched in her hand after she'd ended the call.

'Chobi, you are here, aren't you?'

She touched me softly with her fingers, and I shuddered under the weight of her sadness as I crouched there in the cold glow that shone in through the curtains from the street lights outside.

'Someone . . . someone . . .' I heard her say, and I knew that her connection with someone important had ended. 'Someone help me!'

She kept crying and crying.

And the world kept turning round and round in the endless darkness.

Summer was finally drawing to a close.

Along with it came the call of a new cicada, *kanakanakanakana*. Mimi and I tried to copy it, but we couldn't manage – it just came out as *nyanyanya* or *hyahyahya*.

*She* hadn't been well since that night. She'd cut her long hair short and dyed it a light brown. She looked really pretty. I wished her face would brighten up as much as her hair.

During the day, while she was out, I would visit Jon.

We'd been getting on well lately, and he talked about a lot of things. He knew many things that I didn't, so I learned a lot from him.

To begin with, I'd been upset that he never seemed to listen to me, but once I realized he was a bit deaf, we became firm friends.

'Hi, Jon, I'm here to see you again.'

'Hey, Chobi. Looking good again today, I see.'

As always, Jon lay inside his kennel with his head resting on his paws crossed in front of him. He looked just like a garden ornament.

'I'm worried about *her*. I really want to fill the gap in her heart,' I would often say.

'Chobi, like I said, it's not possible,' he answered sadly. 'After all, neither of you remember, do you?'

'Remember what?'

'When life was created. I do, and that's why I'm not lonely.'

'When life was created?'

'That's right. Why do you think animals are male and female? Have you ever wondered about that, Chobi?'

It was in the nature of things for there to be male and female, and I'd never given it a second thought. I told him this honestly and he gave a big sigh.

'Before women and men became separate, there was no loneliness. It was a happy time, you know.'

'So it isn't possible to be happy any more?'

'That's not what I'm saying.' He looked off into the distance. 'Life split into two sexes in order to survive.'

'Really?'

'Life became stronger after the sexes were separated.'

'I find that hard to believe.' I recalled the sight of her crying. She wasn't strong at all.

'You could call it the power to love, the power to need others. This power we gained in exchange for loneliness makes a species stronger.'

I didn't always understand what Jon said, but I was glad if her loneliness and sadness weren't all for nothing.

'I remember the happy time when there was no loneliness. Everything was one at that time. To begin with, our world was simple, before it became gradually more complicated. You see, in the beginning there were very few elements forming the world. It took an incredibly long time for stars to keep forming and dying, and more elements were made inside the shrinking stars. The molecules created at that time are still flowing in our blood, even now. And in our cells, the surface of the earth, and that train you love so much, Chobi. I remember this.'

'Do I have things made from the stars in me too?'

'Yes, you do, Chobi. Your owner does too. It's because you don't remember this that you are both lonely hearts,' Jon said.

That night, after listening to Jon, I gazed up at the sky. If what Jon had said was true, we had all been one once.

She came over to me and crouched by my side.

According to Jon, the light of each and every shining star was the same light as that of the sun. The very thought made me dizzy, and details seemed less important.

I wished I could tell her what Jon had said.

We sat side by side, gazing at the stars.

I could hear the sound of the train going over the elevated tracks in the distance. The sound of what drives the world. With us on it, this planet keeps turning.

The season had changed again and it was now winter.

It was the first time I'd ever seen snow, but I felt I knew it from long, long ago.

When I breathed, the windowpane fogged up and I couldn't see out. The light from an automatic vending machine in the street blurred on the misted glass. It looked beautiful.

Snow was piling up around the traffic lights and the postbox, and everything looked fresh and dazzling.

*

The sun rose late in winter, and it was still dark when it was time for her to leave the apartment.

From behind, her head with its short hair looked as round as a cat's. When she wrapped herself up in her thick coat, she looked even more like a cat.

'See you later, Chobi,' she said, stroking the top of my head like she always did, then opening the heavy metal door. The smell of cold air and snow came blowing in.

She put on her heavy boots and stepped outside. Shutting the door with a loud clang, she turned the key and went down the outside stairs.

I pictured her blowing white breath on her thin, bare fingertips.

Clouds drifted across the sky above her as she walked in the snow, while snowflakes floated around her.

I waited for her in our apartment.

I'd been able to leap on to the table in one move for quite a while now. The tabletop was decorated with pictures she'd cut out of magazines.

I glanced out of the window. A black pylon towered like a giant over the snow-covered townscape.

The snow was absorbing every noise.

My ears pricked up as her train passed by. The sound of a beating heart that made the world go round.

This one unchanging pulse in the ever-changing world was a source of comfort to me.

I couldn't do anything about her problems.

I just lived my days at her side.

# 2

FIRST BLOSSOMING

It was a long, summer's afternoon and the large, over-grown camphor tree filled the neighbourhood with its fragrance.

Beneath the tree, in an apartment that got little sunlight, a young woman was thinning paints with an oil that smelled of pine resin. She sat before a tight-stretched white canvas, took a deep breath, and closed her eyes.

It was a quiet residential area, but this run-down old building was noisy even during the day with residents playing instruments to their hearts' content, the sports commentary blaring on the radio, and the rusty old stairs creaking. On top of that, there was this strange smell, so normal cats wouldn't come anywhere near the place.

We cats dislike strong or strange smells, and we hate noisy places. That meant there wouldn't be any other cats around to bully me, so I could relax.

And I was also a bit deaf, so this level of noise didn't bother me in the slightest.

The apartment building was surrounded by an unkempt garden. The big camphor tree was in this garden, and I was sitting on one of its branches, watching her.

She was still glaring at the white canvas, motionless. I'd only been born at the beginning of that summer and didn't yet know much about humans, but I couldn't help thinking that staring at a blank canvas like this wasn't normal.

Finally, she made a move. With one swift gesture, she painted a thick black line in the middle of the canvas.

A tingling feeling ran through my body, my tail snapping upright from the sheer power of her movement.

She was incredible. She was short and slight and her hair was a weird colour, but she was awesome.

She continued to layer paints on the canvas until the sun went down and the street lights came on. A scene I'd never seen before began to emerge.

Suddenly, she looked over at me. Her gaze was so sharp it transfixed me and I couldn't move.

'Mimi!'

That's what she called me. Until then, people had only ever called me things like 'Shoo!' or 'Thief!' or 'Damn stray!'

She didn't try to chase me away, and even gave me some food. The canned fish in oil was really delicious, and what's more, I now had a name, so I was very happy.

I would call myself Mimi from now on, I decided.

That cat was the spitting image of the cat I'd had when I was in elementary school.

Little Mimi – completely white, and such an attention seeker. She would always sit in the upstairs window waiting for me to come home from school. Whenever I sat at my desk sketching, she would come and sit on top of the white drawing paper, demanding my attention. She would roll across the paint while it was still wet, and get all sorts of colours all over her pure white fur.

She was so cute at mealtimes, when she would sit on the sideboard mewing, trying to join in our conversation.

Come to think of it, Mum and Dad were still together when we had Mimi. We all still ate breakfast together. I would talk about school and they would both listen to me. They would laugh with me about things that were funny, and get angry about things that had hurt me.

At some point, though, we started eating meals separately and hardly ever talked. Now Mum and Dad were living apart with their new partners.

After finishing school, I decided to leave home and start living on my own. Mum and Dad were against it, but they were doing as they pleased and I wanted to be selfish too.

The apartment I lived in now was old and dirty, but it was rent-free. Or rather, I was supposed to pay it all back only when I started making money, thanks to the fact that my landlady was my grandma on Mum's side. I always got everything dirty when I painted anyway, so the state of the place really let me off the hook.

*

I'm now studying art at the technical college. I'd started taking classes there during my last year of high school to help prepare for the entrance exam for an art course at university, but I'd failed it. I'd lost interest in retaking the exam, and was wondering whether to look for a job instead. Lots of people considered an art course to be an easy way to get a degree, since you spent all your time painting and didn't have to study much. That meant it was highly competitive, and it was all about accepted technique. By the time I'd realized that, it was too late.

All those guys who were too lazy to study for an entrance exam and thought they might be able to get by with painting traditional pictures made things difficult for students like me who really did have talent.

I knew my paintings were brilliant. Not that I got any praise from the teachers, who were all graduates of art courses and failed artists themselves. They just made you practise the established methods over and over again.

The cat that reminded me so much of my old Mimi was really fascinated by my pictures. If even cats saw it, why couldn't those guys? To be perfectly frank, nobody around me could paint as well as I did.

Having been blessed with this amazing talent, I figured I could put up with some misfortune. Like being so short, for example, or having ruined my hair by dyeing it, or failing the university entrance exam.

And I believed things like happiness and misfortune depended on how you saw things. The fact that my parents had both had affairs and split up was a misfortune, but it had led to me being financially stable and able to live on my own for free. Failing to get into university was a misfortune, but then I was happy because it meant I could work out what I wanted to do with my life. I would be able to make a living from my painting.

When I was painting, various thoughts came and went in my mind, and before I knew it, I was so engrossed that I only saw my work.

Today my brush moved smoothly, probably because I had an audience in that white cat. By way of thanks, I gave her a can of the tuna that I usually have for dinner. Seeing her gobble it up like that reminded me of Mimi. She loved tuna too.

For a moment, I considered keeping her. It wasn't expressly against the rules to keep pets here, but none of the other residents seemed to have any. They were all too self-indulgent or too poor, or both. None of them looked like the sort of people responsible enough to take care of an animal.

Having said that, art materials cost money and I never had enough, so I couldn't afford a cat.

Her name was Reina. I found that out when she introduced herself to me. I'd never met a human who introduced themselves to a cat before.

She always smelled weird. The smell of alcohol, the smell of paints, the smell of perfume, the smell of foreign spices, sometimes even the smell of tobacco, though she didn't smoke herself.

She was unpredictable, and some days she fed me, others not.

When she didn't feed me, it was because she was so absorbed in her painting. During those times, there was nothing for it but to beg for food from someone in another apartment, or to filch a bit from somewhere. There was a dripping tap in the wilderness of a garden behind the apartment block where I could always drink clean water.

Mostly, she fed me some of whatever she was eating herself, and sometimes it was delicious, but there were also things I never wanted to eat again. When she was in a good mood, she would give me proper canned cat food.

She fed me, but I wasn't her cat.

'I'm sorry, but I can't keep you,' she told me when we first met. 'After all, cats die.'

I would too, I thought. Lots of cats died young. I was all white and the runt of the litter, plus I was a bit deaf. I'd often had close escapes with cars, nearly getting run over, or hadn't noticed another cat approaching until it was too late.

'But I guess it's a cat's job to die,' she said, and laughed.

Mimi must have been a cat she'd lost, which meant I was Mimi the Second.

Reina said she was selfish, so she'd feed me when she wanted to. And not just that. I was taking a nap in the shade on some cool concrete when she suddenly grabbed me by the scruff of the neck and gave me a bath in a washbasin.

'You really are snow-white, aren't you? A beauty!'

I'd been thinking I really was going to die, but when she called me a beauty, I cheered up. I was happy she'd praised me.

I really like her.
She's so strong!

Puddles created by the evening shower reflected the blue sky.

I was on my way home from the college, thinking about what to have for dinner, when I heard someone calling me from behind. It was Masato from my class.

'What's up?' I asked, making a show of stopping.

'Everyone in the class is talking about going to the swimming pool this summer . . . it'd be great if you'd join us.'

He always spoke hesitantly, mumbling his words. He was so spineless.

'No, thanks,' I said shortly, and started walking again.

'Ah. Like I thought . . .' he said with an air of regret, following a few paces behind me. 'Well, it doesn't matter.'

Doesn't it now?

'Are you really going to drop out of the course?'

I nodded. 'I'm gonna get a job.' I hadn't told my parents yet, but I'd made up my mind.

'Seriously?' Masato said, wide-eyed. 'If you're on the course just for the entrance exam, you could always do design or something instead.'

'It's not that.' I was getting irritated.

'Why, then?'

'I want to paint, but painting to pass an entrance exam is just meaningless,' I said.

'I guess. I feel the same way,' he admitted so readily that I was wrong-footed. 'But I'm sure you'll pass anyway.'

'Oh?' I was quite pleased he'd said that. I made an effort to keep up my stony expression.

'And you know what? It's a wave pool . . .'

So he hadn't given up yet. 'Stop bothering about me and go and do some painting!' I was getting really annoyed now. 'It's not the moment for someone so crap at it to be messing around!'

'But the teacher said that life experiences are important too,' Masato said, without appearing to be offended.

'You can hardly call splashing around in water a life experience.'

'You never know, it might be the beginning of an earth-shatteringly great love affair.'

'Give me a break.'

I often heard about classmates getting together and breaking up. They might have thought they were experiencing something special, but their affairs all just looked silly to me.

'Your mind's made up, isn't it?' Masato said wryly. 'You'll submit something for the autumn art festival, won't you?'

The art festival competition had an age limit, so it was a gateway to success for young people who wanted to pursue fine art. Time-wise, I had to start painting for it now.

'Yeah, planning to.'

'Good luck!'

'You too.'

His eyes grew wide in surprise. Maybe the wimp hadn't thought of submitting anything himself.

We reached the station and went our separate ways.

I was abandoned as a kitten.

There were five of us in the litter, and to begin with, we were pampered by Mum and the couple who owned us. Lots of people came to visit us and Mum was a nervous wreck, but I was in high spirits, loving all the attention.

It didn't last long, though. All my siblings were taken away, but nobody wanted me and I was dumped just like that. I was the smallest, would often throw up my milk, and I was hard of hearing, so they didn't find me so adorable. I was the weakest of us all.

It's natural for the weakest cats to disappear first.

I wanted to be strong in front of Reina. That's why I chose not to move into her apartment and slept in the camphor tree. Nasty bugs and cats avoid camphor trees, so it was quite comfortable there.

I didn't want to rely on her feeding me, and I wanted to catch my own prey. If I could hunt, I'd be even stronger. I wanted to be able to show Reina I could be independent, too.

Reina apparently had other territories as well. She would leave the apartment in the morning and come home again in the evening. Sometimes she stayed home until the afternoon, other times she was out from early morning until late at night. Sometimes she didn't come home at all. Those nights, my heart ached.

Once, she was away from home for several days and I got so worried that I went out looking for her. That's when I met Chobi.

Chobi had beautiful white fur all over, just like me. I loved him the moment I saw him. I was scared of male cats because they usually got all pushy, but he was different and really easy-going.

'Yo!' he greeted me when he saw me.

'Is this your territory?'

'I guess.'

My heart started pounding. I'd come into another cat's territory without realizing it. 'So are you going to chase me out?'

'You're just a kitten. No need.'

'What a gentleman.' He was pretty strange for a cat.

'I'm Chobi,' he introduced himself.

'I'm Mimi.'

I went closer so that I could smell him. We both sniffed each other. Chobi had a human smell on him.

'Are you someone's pet?'

'Yep. I'm her cat.'

'Her cat?'

'I don't know her name. I don't care what she's called. But she's my girlfriend.'

'Weird.'

'Maybe so.'

'It's weird that you don't know your own girlfriend's name,' I said, feeling a bit jealous.

'A name is just a name. Even if you call a cat a dog, a cat is still a cat, right?'

Nobody had ever talked to me like this and it felt kind of strange. I wanted to stay talking longer, but then I spotted Reina. She was carrying a big white bag, and inside it I could make out a distinctive round object – a can of cat food. I was in for a treat.

'Can we meet again?'

'Probably.'

'Not probably. Definitely!' I wanted the cat food, but I also wanted to meet Chobi again.

'Okay, let's meet.'

'That's a promise, right? Definitely a promise!'

I got him to promise and I left.

When I ran up to Reina and miaowed, she smiled at me.

'Mimi, did you smell the can and come to check it out?'

I felt happy and rubbed the back of my head against her calf. But then it occurred to me that Chobi did the same thing to his girlfriend, and that hurt.

After that, Chobi and I met up almost every day. Now and then I treated him to one of Reina's meals.

He was useless at hunting, though. In fact, he was so bad at it that a normal cat would have lost interest in him. But my mother had been bad at it too, so it struck me as kind of cute somehow. I'd actually wanted him to teach me how to do it. I hoped that I'd eventually be able to catch my own

prey and take it to Reina. I wanted to pay her back some day
for all the food she gave me.

I was deep into my painting in the steaming summer heat
when I suddenly got the urge to hose myself down from
head to toe with water. The air conditioner was creating a
terrible din, and it wasn't making the room any cooler at all.

Those guys were probably at the pool right now . . . I
shook my head defiantly, and forced out any sense of regret.
No, I was dedicating my life to art.

After a while, I heard some familiar footsteps outside the
window. It was Mimi. She'd brought a guest with her
today – another white cat who looked just like her, and who
was wearing a collar. If he has an owner, he should get his
owner to feed him, I thought, but then for all I knew Mimi
was getting fed elsewhere too. Okay, I would treat them
both to a can of tuna.

Just at the sound of the can opening, Mimi got thor-
oughly excited. As soon as I put the plate of tuna down, she
dug in, chomping contentedly. Her guest tentatively tried a
bite, then showed surprise.

As I watched them chewing together companionably, my
irritation began to subside, and I decided to join them in a
snack. I took out a rock-hard Häagen-Dazs from my over-
cooled freezer.

'I might be dressed in rags, but my heart is made of

brocade. My home is a scuzzy old apartment, but only Häagen-Dazs ice cream will do, I'll have you know!'

I often chatted with Mimi. She glanced at me while still stuffing herself with tuna. It might have sounded like I was just chatting to myself, but it was nice to have someone to talk to while I ate, even if it was just a cat. There wasn't anyone on my wavelength at college and it's stupid to hang out with people you don't get along with, so I always had lunch on my own.

I sat down by the window and studied my apartment. I currently had three paintings on the go. The ones I finished got shoved into a cupboard.

A sofa bed, a small bookcase, a clothes box. A sink and a portable gas burner. A small refrigerator. Art materials and a supply of instant noodles. My little world. Underneath the paint-stained carpet, the tatami mats and floorboards were soft and creaky, and I could hear people speaking two apartments away.

My apartment was small and dirty, but I liked it.

Reina's eyes had a feverish glint to them. I loved her strength, her super super-confident behaviour. I'd never be like that.

She wielded her paintbrush without hesitating, adding more and more layers. The paint's smell gently wafted up. Funny how it was slightly different depending on the colour.

I miaowed as loudly as I could, but I couldn't get her to hear me.

Finally she noticed. 'What's up, Mimi? You hungry?'

She opened a can of tuna for me, keeping one eye on the painting. The fish was a bit salty, but I couldn't afford to be fussy.

I was scoffing down the food when I got the feeling I was being watched, and looked up to see a hawk. It had the silhouette typical of a bird of prey. I instinctively recoiled and toppled off the windowsill.

Reina saw me and fell about laughing. 'Did I paint it *that* well?'

Of course it wasn't a real hawk, it was in her painting, and when I took a closer look, I saw it was just thick layers of paint. In the moment, though, I'd honestly thought it was real. I'd never seen a hawk in my life, but my instinct had warned me of a dangerous creature's presence.

Reina really was incredible.

I was proud to be at her side.

I carried on painting until the sun rose and, having gone to sleep so late, it was well after noon by the time I woke up.

I had a quick lunch at the beef bowl place on the main road, then went back to my apartment. As I was going in, I bumped into the girl from the apartment next to mine. She worked nights and always wore thick make-up.

'Reina, you have a guest waiting for you,' she said in her regional accent that I liked so much.

'Oh, right. Thank you!'

I bobbed my head in a bow. It was very unusual for me to have a visitor. Who could it be? For some reason, Masato's face sprang to mind. Although there was no way it would be him.

A woman was waiting outside my apartment. I didn't recognize her right away because she was dressed differently than usual.

'Welcome home.' It was the quietly spoken woman from the academic affairs office at the technical college.

'Oh, hi, Miyu. What's up?' I asked.

Miyu smiled shyly. 'Well, I live near by, so . . . To be honest, I shouldn't really be visiting a student at home, but . . .'

She sounded unusually embarrassed, but I had a pretty good idea why she'd come.

'No problem,' I told her as I unlocked my apartment door. 'Come on in. It's small and dirty, though.'

I wasn't just being glib. If I'd known she was coming over, I'd have tidied up a bit, but it was too late for that.

Miyu saw my room and gulped – not from shock at the state of the place, but because she'd caught sight of the painting I was working on.

'Wow! That's a masterpiece.'

I was thrilled by her reaction. I mentally punched the air. *Yes!* 'I don't know when I'll ever finish it, though.'

Mimi was curled up on top of the sofa bed, and opened her eyes to look at Miyu.

'She had the same reaction as you did, Miyu.' I tickled Mimi under her chin.

'Oh, you have a cat?'

'Well, she's not really mine, but she's kind of moved in with me. I suppose she's a stray.'

'She looks pretty settled with you. She obviously trusts you.'

'I guess.'

I washed my hands, then rinsed a couple of glasses and poured some cold barley tea.

'Thank you. I have a cat too.'

'You do?'

'He's really similar to this one, a white cat. But he's male.'

I remembered the white cat Mimi had brought with her once for a tuna meal. That would be an incredible coincidence.

'Um, it seems like you haven't been to college recently.' Miyu changed tack abruptly.

'That's because I haven't.'

Miyu looked at me, then exhaled. 'Look. This isn't an official visit, and I'm only giving you my personal opinion. It's probably not even my place to say this, but . . . I've seen a lot of students in my time, and there's something I really want to tell you.'

I was getting fed up with her roundabout way of talking. 'Just get to the point, will you?'

'Being good at painting is not enough to make your way in the future.'

That hurt.

'I know,' I blurted out. My fingertips were trembling.

'Reina, won't you try the university entrance exam again?' She looked me straight in the eye.

Deep down, part of me had been hoping to hear those

words. But what came out of my mouth didn't reflect how I really felt.

'Doesn't make much difference even if you do go, does it?' I knew that I was just being cynical.

'That's what you say *after* graduating.'

That cut to the quick. Miyu spoke gently, but it really struck a chord.

'You're pretty blunt,' I said, being honest this time.

'You could get a job, but it'll be hard to find time to paint when you're so busy.'

I knew that, too.

'I said I'm fine!'

I knew I had no grounds for saying this and simply didn't want to give in. My voice had become louder, and Mimi was starting to get restless, taken aback by my ferociousness.

'Talent isn't enough to get a foothold in the art world, you know. Regardless of whether it's a good thing or not, if you don't go to university, you'll never get anyone to take you seriously.' Before I could open my mouth, she went on, 'Unless some art critic somewhere discovers you and you get treated as outsider art, that is.'

I knew all that, too.

'Don't worry. With my art I'll be able to get by. Right now I'm painting my entry piece for a competition.'

Miyu laughed.

'What are you laughing at?' I demanded, thinking she was making fun of me.

'Oh, I'm sorry. You're great, Reina. I just thought that if I had your confidence, my life would probably be different.'

Her words had the ring of truth about them. 'What's up? Man problems?'

I'd just hazarded a guess, but she became visibly flustered.

'No, nothing like that . . .'

Seemed I'd hit the nail on the head. She was so easy to read.

'You'll be fine, Miyu. You're a really good person. I mean, you were so worried about me that you came all this way to see me, right? Kindness like that doesn't go unnoticed.'

'I don't know about that . . .'

For some reason I'd ended up trying to cheer *her* up . . . How the heck did that happen? Mimi gave a lazy yawn and curled up on the sofa bed again.

'Well, anyway, I'll think about what you said.'

'Please do. And . . .'

'I'll go to college. One of these days.'

'Thank you.'

She smiled.

The woman who'd been at Reina's place smelled of Chobi. She must be his so-called girlfriend, I guessed.

I'd been feeling upset ever since she'd come over, and I knew it was because of Chobi, but that wasn't all.

Miyu had said I should resit the university entrance exam, but the summer was already coming to an end and I still hadn't decided whether to take the exam or get a job.

The art school arranged for me to spend the last two weeks of the summer break doing an internship. I'd forgotten to apply for one myself.

An internship sounded good, but it seemed to me that all you did was work for free. I felt like blowing them out at first, but I changed my mind when I found out the place I was going to was a design company that even I had heard of. They'd designed logos for popular films and the covers of bestselling manga.

As you might expect of a design office, it was located in a chic part of town some distance from my apartment. And so for the first time in ages, I would be living a regular lifestyle.

I was nervous as hell the first day. I was given the sort of work anyone could do, like taking the minutes at meetings, sticking on address labels, that sort of thing, but at least I could get to see the work of professional designers up close.

It was the first time I'd seen pros at work. Everyone was really quick, and it was impressive to see how many concepts they came up with while I was only doing little chores, but I was happy I could be of use to people like this.

And I was even happier about the lunches. There were so many classy restaurants in the area. Every day the staff would take turns treating me to an expensive lunch, and all the restaurants we went to were amazingly delicious.

This made me realize how badly I usually ate. A delicious meal stimulated the appetite and energy levels. I'd expected

it to be just work with no pay. I initially had zero motiv-
ation, but actually, I found it rewarding.

I'd taken the bait, just like Mimi.

Everyone in the design company was used to having
interns like me, so they took good care of me. The man
they called the Boss especially looked out for me.

My first impression of him was that he wasn't a very nice
guy. Guys that wear aftershave are all jerks – like my dad, for
example. The Boss was young, but there was something
about him that reminded me of Dad.

It seems he was the one who'd decided to take me on as
an intern.

I gave him a portfolio of all my finished work, and he
praised me for it. We went to lunch together, just the two of
us, and he listened attentively as I spoke passionately about
the painting I was currently working on.

'You must show it to me sometime,' he said casually with
a smile.

I'd like him to see it, I thought – the painting that had
taken both Mimi and Miyu by surprise. I was sure he would
be impressed by it.

'Please come any time. My place is pretty dirty, though,'
I said.

I thought he'd come around right away, but work got
really busy so there was no chance of that. Some people
were even staying overnight in the office. Even I, in my own
way, worked hard from morning to evening.

The crunch time before a big deadline was fun, a bit like
the day before the school festival. Of course I wasn't

directly involved, so I was quite relaxed about it all, but they were grateful to me for going out to buy bentos for them, and I was happy to be of use. When I thought about it, I'd never really been of use to anyone before.

'Great job, everyone. Cheers!'

They all raised their glasses in a toast once the project was finished. I was still a minor and was only there at the recommendation of my college, so I decided to be sensible and stick to Coke.

To my delight, the Boss remembered about coming to see my painting. He'd been so busy that I was sure he had forgotten, so I was happy when he asked for my number.

'Be careful of that guy – he's into young women, you know,' one of the designers whispered in my ear later.

Really, some women get so jealous!

It turned out I was wrong about that.

Summer was coming to an end, and my body was beginning to change as I grew from a kitten into an adult female cat.

I was desperate to have Chobi's children, so I decided to try asking him outright.

'Let's get married!'

'Look, Mimi, how many times have I told you? I have a girlfriend.'

That old story again. I wanted to find out once and for all

if it was that woman who had been at Reina's place. What sort of a girlfriend was that?

'I want to meet her.'

'No.'

'Why not?'

'Mimi, I've told you so many times . . . we shouldn't even be talking about this sort of thing until you grow up.'

I was so sad my whiskers, ears and tail all drooped.

Having a human girlfriend was insane. Well, be like that, then.

Still in a sulk, I stomped my way over to Reina's studio.

When I sat in the usual camphor tree and looked into her apartment, I saw she was speaking on the phone to someone.

'Whaaat? Noooo, not at all!'

Her voice was all coquettish, nothing like the way she usually spoke. That wasn't Reina! I wanted her to be strong and resolute, not buttering anyone up.

Unbearable rage welled up in me and made me want to attack something. If I tried hunting now, I was sure I'd be able to catch something.

I don't know what came over me, but I felt the need to get away from there. I made my way quickly along unknown fence tops and through unknown thickets. Normally, I would have been too scared to go to any of these places I didn't know, with air that I'd never smelled before, but that day I didn't care.

I was off my guard, and by the time I sensed danger and

realized I'd entered another cat's territory, it was too late. A male cat with piercing eyes stood blocking my way. He was feral, and huge. Just the fact that he clearly had plenty to eat meant that he was strong.

He had a big scar in the black-and-white fur on his side. The tip of his tail, sticking up high, was crooked. In my mind, I called him Kink Tail.

Kink Tail was watching me as if to appraise me. When I took a step forward, his eyes told me not to get any closer.

'Catch it for me. Please?' Even I was taken aback by how sweet my own voice sounded.

'What?' he asked dubiously.

A long-tailed bird was pecking at the gravel in the car park. He glanced at it, then silently made a move. He inched his way along the top of the wall towards the bird, then, flexing every muscle in his body, he suddenly leaped off and sank his teeth unerringly into its neck. The bird flapped its wings desperately.

'Wow!' It was so amazing that I was speechless. All my fur stood on end.

As the life drained rapidly from the bird in his mouth, he dropped it in front of me.

'It's no big deal. Birds can't see well at dusk,' he said, like a parent teaching a child. He was quite a bit older than me, I realized.

'I'm Mimi. What's your name?'

'I don't have one.'

'Well, then, can I call you Kink Tail?'

'Do as you like.'

He turned his back and walked off, and instinctively I ran after him. I really am a cat, I thought.

That night, Kink Tail and I tied the knot.

The next day I saw Chobi again. He didn't know anything about what had happened.

There was a cicada with a strange *kanakana* call. We tried imitating it, and when we couldn't, we burst out laughing.

Normally, I asked Chobi to marry me every time I met him, but for the first time, I left without mentioning it. I didn't make him promise to meet me the next day either.

He went back to *her* without saying anything. My tail drooped just thinking about it.

Reina had seemed somewhat elated for several days and wouldn't understand my troubles. For my part, I was still left with a lot of unresolved feelings, and I spent all my time sleeping.

'It looks like I've got a job,' Reina said cheerfully.

'It seems like the Boss in the design office where I interned has taken a shine to me.

'He says I'm talented. I already knew that, but . . .

'It'll be hard work, but I think that company may be worth considering.'

I found her unwavering strength dazzling.

As I listened to Reina chattering on, something occurred to me. Cats all have their own territory. There are small and big territories depending on the cat, but whatever the size, there is only one cat in each.

With humans, there are any number of people jostling for space in the same territory. You might think they all get along fine together, but that's all for show, and in reality, there is just one person controlling any given territory.

Artists like Reina were continually competing for a small territory, and even though they fought hard, only the strongest would survive. Reina was really strong, so she hadn't been beaten yet.

Little by little, the season turned into autumn, and a cool breeze started to blow.

The trees left to grow wild around Reina's apartment began to change colour. Only the camphor tree remained green, and its round berries started to ripen.

As I stepped over golden and reddish-bronze leaves, I took in a deep breath. My body was getting quite big and Reina laughed at me when I got stuck in the gap I always used to enter her apartment.

Then there was a big autumn typhoon that was so fierce it felt like the rain and wind would reduce everything caught up in it to rubble.

That night, Reina took me up to her apartment and kept me close to her. I relived the fear I'd felt as a kitten as I listened to the apartment creaking and objects banging against the storm shutters, but Reina remained unflappable, absorbed in her painting.

I didn't sleep a wink all night and the next morning, when

I glimpsed the clear blue sky, I instinctively knew that something had changed irrevocably.

It was a fat cat, round like a barrel, who informed me of Kink Tail's death.

The cat introduced himself as Kuro, and then said, 'I hear you were close to him?'

'Him?'

'The guy with a kink in his tail, here. You knew him, right?'

'Kink Tail?'

'Was it you who gave him that name? Well, then, it's definitely you. He was quite taken with it, you know. It's not often that ferals get to have a name, I guess.' He was quiet for a moment, then said, 'He's dead.'

Kink Tail was dead. I quietly took this in.

'Aren't you surprised?'

'I had a feeling about it.' Given how much the world had changed, I'd been expecting something like this.

'That means his territory is yours.'

'What?' Now, that did surprise me. 'Why me? Aren't there any other cats after it?'

'That's how things work in this town,' Kuro said, as if it were obvious. 'Well, I'll be going, then,' he added, turning his back on me.

'Er, thank you.'

I'd meant to thank him for informing me, but he misunderstood.

'It wasn't my decision. If you're going to thank anyone, thank Jon.'

'Jon?'

'He's a dog.'

With a swift movement that belied his bulk, he disappeared.

I didn't feel sad. I was just very, very sleepy. I slept in Reina's apartment for a while. She wasn't home, but then she often wasn't.

After a while, Kuro came back. 'Oi, it's about time you patrolled your territory,' he said, and went away again.

I stepped slowly around Kink Tail's territory. It was a dilapidated factory covered in rusty tin. There was an almost completely dried-up canal full of rubbish, and endless concrete walls blackened by exhaust fumes. It was bleak. This lonely site was where Kink Tail had spent his entire life.

A single peach-coloured cosmos was blooming in a corner of the empty car park. And then it hit me: that must have been where Kink Tail died.

I was overcome with a sadness that felt like it would tear me apart.

I wanted Reina to comfort me. But I also had the feeling I shouldn't see her.

I had grown big, but I was still basically a kitten, and if Reina ever realized I was a weak, useless cat, she would probably abandon me. Just like my first owner did.

Reina wasn't home today either. She'd probably gone to that place where she was an intern or something. That suited me well.

I curled up under the eaves of her apartment and, enveloped in the faint smell of paint, I slept and slept and slept.

★

I was woken up by the sound of a car. It was already completely dark.

I could hear Reina's voice inside the apartment, and felt happy. I was getting hungry. I scratched at the shutters. She normally came right out to see me, but didn't show any sign of doing so this time.

The bastard never was interested in my paintings, only in my body. He didn't even look at my work, unlike Miyu when she came over.

Now that I think about it, he'd probably been like that from the start and I just hadn't wanted to admit it. I'd wanted to believe that he'd spotted talent in me.

He'd given me a lift home, and I'd listened elatedly as he strung together sentences of vacuous praise.

I was so stupid. And now he'd pushed me down on the sofa bed. The smell of the aftershave he was wearing made me feel like throwing up.

This was not at all what I'd had in mind.

I knew exactly what the bastard was after. And to make matters worse, I'd invited him over.

*Be careful of that guy – he's into young women, you know.*

I realized now that the woman in the design office had been sincere in her warning.

It's part of the job. If I do what the bastard wants, he'll

probably give me a job. It's part and parcel of human relations. Maybe I should just go along with it . . .

I would never forgive myself for thinking that, however briefly. I absolutely couldn't deceive myself.

I was enveloped in his sickly-sweet smell as he began running his hands over my body. I was so scared and ashamed that I was letting him do it.

'You're so cute!'

The way he said this was so creepy that I got goosebumps.

'Stop!' His hands didn't stop. 'Get your hands off me!'

Now my voice came from my belly and I could move again. I grabbed the nearest thing and hit him in the face with it. It was the jacket he'd been wearing.

As he recoiled, I tried to get off the bed, but he held me from behind.

'I said, don't touch me!'

I twisted my body and, aiming for his solar plexus, elbowed him hard.

Bullseye. He fell off the bed, knocking over piles of books and paintings.

'Come on, Reina. Surely you don't mean that.'

His flippant smile was so disgusting I couldn't stand it. I no longer felt scared.

'I mean it all right. Get out!'

I grabbed a magazine lying near by and threw it in his face.

'Seems like there's been a misunderstanding . . . Shall we talk about it?'

That smiling face couldn't deceive me any more. It made me sick that I'd ever tried to suck up to a guy like this.

One of the legs had fallen off the easel holding my painting, and I grabbed it. Realizing I was serious, he backed out of the apartment. I sank down on to the floor, still holding the easel leg.

The door opened again. For a moment, I thought the bastard had come back, and I tensed. But then the girl from next door poked her head in.

'Reina, are you okay?'

Her heavily made-up face and soft voice were so reassuring I almost wept. The tears were about to spill out, and that fuelled my rage. How dare that asshole make me cry?

'Wait!'

I slipped my feet into some sandals and ran outside. The Boss was still there, leaning on his car and smoking a cigarette. His beloved wheels – French, I think the car was. The way he was posing was so offensive.

He glanced at me, grinning. What was he expecting me to say after all that?

'Wait, you bastard!'

Clocking the full extent of my fury, he hastily got into the car. I kicked the door as hard as I could. It crunched pathetically and a dent appeared.

The residents of the other apartments came out to see what all the noise was about.

The Boss stepped on the accelerator and sped off. He must have been driving erratically, as horns sounded here and there.

'Yo, Reina!' the girl next door called, mimicking the appreciative audience calls at kabuki performances.

There were a few hoots from the others, then they all broke into a round of applause.

'This isn't a show!' I barked, before turning on my heel and going back to my apartment.

It still smelled of the bastard. I was angry with myself as much as I was with him. What a fool I'd been.

I opened the window to let in some fresh air.

Mimi came in. She quietly snuggled up to me, and her warmth was the best balm.

'Mimi, stay with me, please.'

She slept with me that night. I didn't want to think about anything for a while.

The season was changing and it was almost winter.

Instead of painting in her studio, Reina was more often doing other things – reading a book, making her own fruit liqueurs, crafting. She was the sort of person who couldn't sit still and was constantly busy, but she wasn't painting.

She got the kotatsu out, and I spent more and more time curled up inside its warmth. I was so sleepy I couldn't keep my eyes open.

The second semester started.

I'd missed so much college and hadn't been studying or keeping up with my class work at all, so I couldn't hand in anything decent. I hadn't even looked at any assignments during the break.

I fell asleep in class and the teacher told me to get out, so I did.

I was sitting outside the college drinking some juice when Miyu came along. It felt like ages since I'd seen her.

'Thanks for coming in.' She clinked her cup of coffee against my can of juice.

'I wanted to see you, Miyu.'

She laughed, but I meant it. I'd sent an email to everyone I'd met in the design office telling them what had happened with the Boss, but I hadn't said anything about it at college. I didn't even know whether Miyu had heard about it or not.

'So you didn't enter the competition?' Miyu said, and I remembered the deadline had passed. 'Masato was the only one from here who entered. You know, the guy in your class.'

So he'd entered, had he?

'He got a prize in that other competition before the summer, too. And one of the judges, Mr Kiriya, has taken him on.'

Wow, the guy hadn't wasted any time . . .

'Well, how about that?' I said. I wanted to mean it, but I had to force a smile.

'You should try your best too, Reina.' She hadn't meant it nastily, but her words hurt.

'Right.' I let out a deep breath. 'You know what? I've learned something about myself. I always believed I was talented. I made the big mistake of believing all the old men who fuss over me. I've still got a ways to go.'

Miyu listened to me in silence.

'Sure, you're just a little fledgling!' a voice boomed suddenly behind me, and I turned round.

'Kamata-sensei.'

He was an old-timer who taught part-time. He had a pack of cigarettes in his hand.

'Don't butt into our conversation!' I said, glaring at his thinning hair. Should I pull it out for him? I was well aware of my own inadequacy.

'But the fact you've realized it yourself means that there's a glimmer of hope for you yet,' he said, and quickly retreated to the smoking corner.

That was probably the best form of encouragement, but it didn't help cheer me up at all.

Masato had been working on his painting all along! And I hadn't done anything.

Reina was lying down and I snuggled up to her.

'He beat me . . . No, wait. I didn't lose; it was never even a contest. I didn't submit anything.'

She stroked me.

'What will become of me now? Painting is my only saving grace, Mimi. Everything – and I mean everything – always comes back round. The words I threw at a guy who I thought was beneath me – you have no talent, give up now . . .'

She shivered.

'Help me! I hate myself so much.'

I gently licked away the teardrops running down her cheeks. They were warm and tasted of her life.

Reina was losing her strength. For the first time in ages, I thought of Chobi.

It had been a long time since I'd last seen Chobi. He was smaller than I remembered, probably because I'd grown so big.

I felt awkward, but he didn't seem to notice and talked to me like a friend he'd just seen yesterday.

'It's okay, Mimi, don't worry.' He repeated this a number of times.

'How do you know that?' For some reason, whenever I was with him, my voice came out all wheedling.

'No human is always strong, but then no human is weak for ever, either.' Then, looking at my swollen belly, he added, 'Oh, and congratulations!'

I was pregnant – with Kink Tail's kittens.

I was one step ahead of Chobi in becoming an adult. I'd always trusted him completely, but now, somehow, I couldn't. I was feeling terribly apprehensive.

I started making preparations to give birth. It was no longer just me – now it was me plus we. I felt weak and needed to save all my strength for the forthcoming delivery. I was terrified of what was going to happen to my body, and knew I would need all my courage to fend off anyone who attempted to rob me of my kittens – I was in turmoil and didn't even know myself any more.

But one thing I had absolutely clear: I didn't want to be a nuisance to Reina.

Reina was hurting right now, and I didn't want to worry her.

As the birth approached, instinct took over and my actions became automatic.

My instinct knew everything I had to do.

I snuck into the apartment's shared storage shed, and made a nest in a space between the stacked skis and piles of cardboard boxes using scraps of cloth I found here and there. The winter cold was sapping my energy.

When the contractions began, I felt sure that my strength wouldn't last for the whole birth. I was small and deaf, and the weakest of the litter. Just the fact I was becoming a mother didn't change that.

The first kitten was born. I broke the sac and made it breathe. When I heard its little cry, I felt an insurmountable joy. I was so glad it was alive.

'. . . Mimi . . .'

I could hear Kink Tail's voice, but, being hard of hearing, I couldn't make out what he was saying.

'What is it, Kink Tail?'

I wanted to hear what he was saying, so I tried to get closer to him. Suddenly, there were pink cosmos flowers blooming all around me. They smelled so lovely.

But Kink Tail was already leaving.

'Wait . . .'

Just then, a piercing pain ran through me.

'Ow, that huuuurt!!!'

Someone was biting my tail. Kink Tail and the cosmos flowers had vanished. I was in the semi-darkness of the shed. Chobi was beside me – he was the one who had bitten me.

'What are you doing here?'

I was furious with him for violating my territory.

'I'm going to get your owner,' he said calmly.

'You won't do anything of the sort!' I was so angry all the hairs on my body stood on end.

'But you're in danger here,' he said, and dashed off through the snow, ignoring my shouts.

I hadn't been able to stay strong until the end. I didn't know whether the pain was from the contractions or in my mind, but it hurt so much I couldn't stand it.

Reina would never try to save me in this state.

I hadn't seen Mimi lately. Maybe she'd abandoned me too . . . And I even had some cans of food ready to give her!

Something white passed outside the window.

Mimi?

I opened the door to see a white cat wearing a collar. I

recognized him. It was the cat Mimi had brought over some time ago.

The cat ran off as if asking me to follow, so I anxiously went after him.

He took me to the apartment's storage shed. Inside, I found a newly born kitten mewling faintly and Mimi covered in blood.

'Oh no! What on earth should I do?'

I was in shock but I had to do something, and so I began to call whoever came to mind.

The first to answer was Masato.

'I'll be right over,' he said, even though I was incoherent.

Finally, we were back to spring again.

Reina's apartment was overrun with my kittens.

Someone called Masato had taken Reina and me to the vet's, and I'd given birth to the remaining four kittens there. I still had a big scar on my belly. It looked bad, but it was kind of fitting for Kink Tail's companion, I thought.

Reina couldn't take her eyes off my babies.

Don't you dare abandon them!

'Mimi, stop glaring at me like that. I'll make sure they all find good homes, don't worry.'

Reina rang around a lot of contacts and, true to her word, she found lovely people to adopt them. I checked them out one by one. Whenever someone I didn't like came round, I hid my babies from them.

Reina painted a picture of me and my kittens. Whenever I looked at it, I wondered how they were all doing.

And there was one more change. Even after I'd finished raising my kittens, I was once and for all living in Reina's apartment.

I was now officially Reina's cat.

I was *her* cat.

# 3

## SLUMBER AND SKY

I had a huge fight with my best friend, my beloved Mari.

We'd always been besties, ever since elementary school.

We'd met in fourth grade. Mari had been seriously ill and missed school for a whole year, so she was older than me, but that didn't bother us at all.

'When I met you, Aoi, it was like meeting myself,' she told me later. I'd felt the same way, so I was really happy to hear it.

We were inseparable both at school and at home, so it was like we were part of each other's families too. I was an only child, but I really thought of Mari as a sister. No . . . even if I'd had real sisters, I wouldn't have been as close to them as I was to Mari.

Maybe because we were always together, we looked similar and had similar personalities. Even our teachers and parents said they couldn't tell us apart. We were soul sisters.

We had the same favourite class (arts and crafts), favourite foods, TV shows and singers. I'd even been surprised by Mari suddenly humming a tune I already had going around in my head. How come we both had this obscure tune in our heads at the same time, we said, rolling about laughing.

We fancied the same guys, too. The only reason this never became a problem was because we only ever really fancied manga characters.

Whenever we got talking about what was so great about them, where we'd like to go with them, how we'd like to spend time with them, Mari would always start thinking up what they'd say. Mari and I spent our adolescence in this world we'd made for ourselves.

She and I both liked drawing pictures, and together we'd draw our favourite manga characters and send fan letters to the artists. When one of them sent us a New Year's card back (one each!), we jumped for joy.

To begin with, we only drew things to show to manga artists or our parents, but little by little we started to get the urge to make them more sophisticated. Instead of just copying manga characters that other people had drawn, we started drawing characters that we ourselves came up with.

At some point, Mari started inventing stories for me to illustrate. She knew better than I did what I wanted to draw.

We also made photocopies of our manga at the convenience store, stapled the pages together and tried to sell these booklets at manga events, though we never actually sold any.

Even after we finished school and got separate jobs, Mari would always come over to my place after work and we'd talk about our manga and our world.

By then, instead of photocopying our booklets at the convenience store, we were taking them to a printer's to produce proper copies, and gradually they began to sell.

Later, at one of the events, we were approached by a publisher – an editor from a really well-known manga magazine. Somebody had discovered us!

Thinking back now, that's when things started to go wrong.

The editor had asked us to create a manga story for the magazine, but in the end we never did finish it.

One night, we sat facing each other in a chicken fast food shop.

'I'm sorry, Aoi,' Mari said.

I didn't say anything and continued eating sullenly, my fingers covered in grease.

It seemed Mari couldn't come up with any stories. Even though the editor and I had both set deadlines for her, no new ideas were coming. And without Mari's stories, I couldn't draw anything.

Until that point, Mari had always written for me. But now, she had to write stories for some obscure, faceless person called the Reader.

Surely, if she could write stories for me, she could write them for anyone? I thought she was just being lazy, saying she couldn't do it.

She said she didn't feel well, but I thought that was all just an excuse too.

All I could think of was that I finally had the chance to make my debut as a manga artist, and it was slipping through my fingers. I could no longer bear to see Mari. I was beginning to feel angry with all her muttered excuses.

'Drop dead!' I yelled at her.

Mari turned ashen and stayed silent. I would never forget the look on her face at that moment.

And the next day, those awful words I'd hurled at her came to pass.

The coldest, cruellest season of the year had arrived. There was less prey, which meant not enough nutrition or calories, and the cold air mercilessly robbed Kuro of his strength.

The weakest were always the first to perish in winter. Kuro had already survived it numerous times; he couldn't recall exactly how many.

As he started sluggishly to walk, the dense layer of fat under his thick fur-covered skin swayed. The fat might not look good, but it protected him.

Kuro couldn't remember what colour his fur had been originally, although his name suggested it had been black. Now it ranged in colour between black and brown.

He wished he didn't have to patrol his territory in this cold.

'I'm getting old . . .' he murmured, but there weren't any cats around to hear him. Since Kink Tail's death, Kuro had become the strongest feral cat in the neighbourhood. No other cats would hang out with him now.

Being king was lonely, as other cats kept their distance. Occasionally a spirited cat would challenge him for the throne, but would flee after a beating.

Kuro's face was covered in scars, but his back and tail were as smooth as a pet cat's. He'd never shown his back to another cat.

He had a big territory of his own and, on top of that, Jon had asked him to keep an eye on several territories belonging to other cats, too. He was indebted to Jon, so had to do as he was asked.

He didn't have one particular place to eat or sleep – the whole area was his home, as far as he was concerned.

'What to do for lunch . . .'

Various menus rose up in his mind. The canned food that an old woman put out for the cats in the park. The Chinese restaurant he was free to cut through. The rubbish bins with loose lids behind the Italian restaurant. He hadn't had the dry cat food from that house for a while, so maybe he'd go there.

Having made up his mind, Kuro set off.

As he left the station area, the roads became wider and there were fewer tall buildings.

Threading his way through some trees, now bare of leaves, a shrine loomed into view. Behind it were rows of identical prefabricated houses. This kind of landscape, where it all looked exactly the same no matter which turn you took or which road you crossed, made him feel dizzy. That's why other cats rarely came here, he thought.

He was a regular visitor at one of these houses. Having said that, he hadn't been here since the summer – a long time ago. He'd had to keep an eye on territorial skirmishes among some young ferals elsewhere.

Last time he'd been here, the lawns had been green, but recently they'd turned completely brown. The dry grass felt more interesting to step on now, though. After enjoying the feel of it for a while, he climbed up on to a breeze-block wall between houses and jumped on to the plastic roof of a car-port. From there he could reach the upstairs balcony of one of the houses.

Some empty flowerpots, rusty pruning scissors and other gardening tools were scattered on the balcony. An aluminium tray had been placed between the outside air-conditioning unit and some withered succulents.

Kuro jumped on to the air-conditioning unit in an attempt to see inside the room. The curtains over the slid-ing glass door had a large flower pattern on them and were closed. Rubbing his body against it, the glass felt cold.

'*Miaow. Miaow,*' he called sweetly. If any other cat heard him like this, he'd lose his status as boss cat, but it was unlikely there would be any around here.

His paw had left an imprint on the glass. There was dust building up in the corners of the door, too. It looked like it hadn't been opened for some time. The plants on the bal-cony hadn't been tended to either.

Maybe they were away? There had always been two women here when he'd visited before, and they had always given him some food, but . . .

A crow cawed loudly, as if laughing at him, and he felt irritated. Dirty rainwater had puddled in the aluminium tray. It didn't look as though another cat had beaten him to it.

He gave a big yawn and decided to wait a while, reluctant to give up. However, there was no sign of the women – having made the effort to visit after so long, it had come to nothing after all.

Well, it wasn't like he had all day . . . With his stomach rumbling, Kuro set off to look around the next territory.

I was woken up by the crows cawing loudly.

It was hot in my room, and I could feel the sun coming through the thick curtains with the large flower pattern.

I couldn't tell whether it was morning or evening. As I crawled out of bed, I caught sight of myself in the full-length mirror. What a state I was in, wearing the same crumpled pyjamas I'd had on for god only knew how long, and my hair all over the place.

My parents had long since gone to work, and the house was in silence.

I was hungry, and went down to the kitchen.

A sandwich wrapped in clingfilm had been left on the table for me, but I didn't find it very appealing and took a look in the fridge. I found a packet of eclairs. The first bite was delicious, but then the sweetness made me feel sick and I threw more than half of it away.

The crows were still cawing loudly outside. It felt like their numbers were increasing. A gang of them were probably scavenging at the neighbourhood garbage collection point. Someone must have been careless when putting their rubbish out, but I couldn't be bothered to go and check. I never went out any more.

I dragged myself back upstairs.

I threw myself down on the bed, covered my head with the blankets, curled up in a foetal position and went back to sleep.

A bell tinkled.

Little Mari from elementary school days appeared in the room.

The bell was on the colourful thread bracelet tied around Mari's wrist. A misanga, it was called – a friendship bracelet.

Back then they were all the rage, and Mari was really good at plaiting them from embroidery threads. I wasn't very good at it, but she was still always happy when I made one for her. When you broke the misanga, your wish would come true, I recalled.

'Mari, I'm sorry,' I apologized, squeezing her small hand. The little bell tinkled.

'I said it was okay, Aoi. It can't be helped.' She smiled gently at me.

Relieved, I decided I wanted something to drink. Suddenly the scene changed to the kitchen at the first company I'd worked for, and I was holding a glass.

The kitchen was dark and I knew there was something lurking further in. Still, I couldn't leave.

'Aoi!' little Mari called, coming to my rescue. 'I'll be fine, you can run away!'

She jumped into the darkness. I was scared and ran off. I abandoned her.

The scene changed to an empty swimming pool. It was covered in small bathroom tiles and water was trickling into it, and garbage bags were strewn around with raw garbage spilling out of gaping holes.

I'd landed here in this desolate place because I'd abandoned Mari.

'I'm sorry, Mari . . .'

The bell tinkled.

'Aoi!'

I saw Mari sitting on the diving board.

'It's okay to run away, Aoi,' she said with a smile.

'Mari . . .'

Mari had forgiven me. I felt saved, but then the feeling that it was a lie welled up in me. This wasn't how Mari felt. I knew it was a dream to protect myself.

A wet newspaper lying on the bottom of the empty pool rustled and waved as if it were alive.

I heard the cawing of a crow erupt from it and woke up.

I could hear the crows cawing outside.

I'd met Mari in my dream. She was no longer in this world.

'Drop dead!'

The day after I'd shouted this at her, she passed away from heart failure.

My phone had rung and I'd seen Mari's number, but it

had been her mother calling to tell me the news. They'd simply found her with her heart stopped.

She'd always had a weak heart.

But I knew the truth. I was the one who'd killed her.

I'd rushed out of the house to go over to Mari's, but the moment I stepped outside it was as if my own heart had been crushed and I couldn't breathe. Everything went dark before my eyes, as if I had some sort of anaemia, and I couldn't stand up.

I apparently had a common mental illness, or whatever it's called. From that day onwards, I wasn't able to take a single step outside.

As I leaned out over the edge of the kotatsu, Mama crawled out from under it and flopped down on top of the quilt.

Mama was always saying that sleeping under the kotatsu was a great way to warm up. When it got too hot, you could lie outside it on the quilt to cool down, and if you started feeling cold again, you could crawl right back under it.

'Mama, look!' I called.

Her whiskers pricked up, and she looked directly at me.

I'm Mama's baby, and my name is Cookie. Reina gave me that name because I have chocolate-coloured stripes on my white fur that apparently make me look like a marbled cookie. I have no idea what that is, but I'm sure it's something nice.

'I'm gonna jump!' I told her, but I had to prepare myself actually to do it. I paced back and forth across the tabletop, sticking my face over the edge, then pulling back. Gradually, I summoned the courage to jump down.

Finally, I launched myself off the edge.

*Poff!* I landed next to Mama on the quilt.

'I did it! It's fun!'

'Wow, that's great, Cookie,' Mama said. 'Well done!'

She grabbed me and started licking me all over. Mama's grooming tickled and felt good. I started purring.

'You know, I'm soon gonna be able to jump from a much, much higher place!' I said, rubbing the back of my head on Mama.

'Of course you will.'

'I'll jump from the ceiling! From the roof! From anywhere!'

I was sure I'd be able to do it.

Even in this apartment there were plenty of places I could jump from — from Reina's painting tools, from the pile of magazines, from the open cupboard filled with artwork. I would conquer them all, together, one by one, with Mama.

'Okay, let's practise,' Mama said and started licking me again.

My four siblings had all gone to new homes. I was the only one left in Reina's apartment. I was the smallest and was always getting sick, so no one wanted to take me. I was sad to be told I wasn't wanted, but I was happy to be able to stay with Mama.

I was practising jumping with Mama when there was a sudden cold draught and Reina entered the apartment.

When I got home, Mimi came over to me with Cookie trotting along behind her.

Mimi sniffed me, then rubbed the back of her head against my calf.

'Do I smell of outside?' I asked her.

Cookie was copying Mimi and sniffing me. Kittens are just the cutest, I have to say. My determination wavered as I watched Cookie, but I couldn't allow myself to be carried away by this feeling.

I took Cookie and Mimi back to the kotatsu.

'I found someone who wants to take Cookie,' I told them.

Mimi's fur was bristling, so I guessed she'd understood what I'd said. She probably wanted to look after her smallest, weakest kitten for ever. But of course, since I lived alone, keeping two cats wasn't really an option. I was at college during the day and was going to take the entrance exam to study art at university, so I'd have to be away for that too.

'It's in this neighbourhood, Mimi, so you'll be able to see Cookie whenever you want to.'

Ignoring me, Mimi grabbed Cookie by the scruff of the

neck and dragged her under the kotatsu. *Miaow!* Cookie
cried from inside.

Mimi came out again on her own and took a swipe at my
leg. This baby is still too young to be on her own, she
seemed to be saying.

The next day, Cookie's new owner came over. She was a
woman who lived near by. My grandmother had found her.
I really did owe Granny so much.

The woman was aged somewhere between Granny and
my own mum, and she had great dress sense for her age.

I looked at the gift she'd brought me and burst out laughing. It was a box of cookies.

'That's the kitten's name – Cookie!'

'Oh, really?' She tittered politely. 'In that case, I'll call her
that too.'

'You're free to give her a new name if you like.'

'But Cookie's a cute name. I like it.'

I was glad that she seemed so nice.

'I heard you had a cat before?' I asked as I poured the tea,
just to make sure.

'When my daughter was little . . . must be around ten or
twelve years ago, maybe. My daughter cried when it died,
and I decided not to get another cat after that.'

'I'm relieved that it's not your first time.'

I put Cookie's favourite blanket and a bag of litter into
the brand-new cat basket the woman had brought with her.
Cookie sniffed the cage curiously and went in of her own
accord. She was no trouble, this kitten.

The woman squatted down to face Mimi. 'I'm taking your daughter with me.'

Mimi glared at her hatefully. I hurriedly picked her up. She was really angry, with her tail all fluffed up.

'I'm so happy that you're coming with me, Cookie,' the woman said to Cookie, who was sitting blankly in the basket.

Mimi sprang from my arms and began ferociously to attack the scratch pad, as though venting the feelings she couldn't control.

I gave the woman details of which food Cookie liked and about toilet training, and then she left, taking Cookie with her.

*Miaow!* Mimi cried. 'I'll come to see you, Cookie!'

*Miaow, miaow!* Cookie cried. 'Make sure you do, Mama! Promise me!'

That's what it seemed they were saying to each other, I thought.

The last kitten had finally left home.

'She's gone, I'm afraid,' I said, giving Mimi's back long, gentle strokes.

It sure is quiet here . . .

My former home had always been lively, and Reina and Mama had been there to care for me. But here, the woman who had taken me away from them, and her husband, too, always left home early and didn't come back until late at night.

When I first arrived, I was lonely and cried, but after a while I got used to being on my own and my urge to explore grew.

For a while I played at going up and down the stairs. There hadn't been any at Reina's place and I discovered they were quite fun.

Then I drank some water, ate some crunchy cat food, and decided to look for somewhere to sleep. I wanted a sunny spot, so I went to check things out upstairs.

There was a door slightly ajar, so I went in and then almost had a heart attack.

A woman was sitting there in the semi-darkness. Her long hair was tied back, and she was wearing the same sort of clothes that Reina wore to sleep in. The sun's rays shone faintly through the curtains with a large flower pattern covering the window.

My fur stood on end and I jumped back, landing on all fours with a thud.

Disturbed by the sound, she turned slowly to me. 'Go away!'

'Who are you?' I blurted out.

'Go away!' she said again. Just that.

The decor in her room was similar to Reina's apartment, although there were more books and things here.

I went closer to get a better smell. She smelled of prey. The smell of the hunted, declining and weak.

She touched me. The spot she touched stung, as if her fingers were transmitting her pain.

*Caw!* came a loud screech outside the window and again I jumped back, landing on all fours. There was some rustling, and then the silhouette of a large bird appeared on the other side of the curtain.

I panicked and began to run round and round the room, looking for somewhere to hide – anywhere would do! I dashed at full pelt under the desk, behind the heater and between the piles of magazines.

'Stop that!' she cried, her voice hoarse.

I scrambled up to the highest shelf and puffed up my tail.

'You're messing up my room!' She covered her face with both hands and burst into tears.

I wondered why she was crying. Then I realized the bird's silhouette had gone. That had been a close call. I started grooming myself to calm down.

I found a pretty thread tangled around my paw – a loop with a silver bell on it. It must have caught on me as I was running around.

I padded my way down off the shelf and strolled over to her. The bell tinkled as I moved. So annoying!

'Hey, can you get this thing off me?'

She stopped crying and looked at me, then grabbed at the thread with the bell and started crying again, even harder than before. I had no idea what that meant.

'You found it! Thank you!'

She gave me a tight hug, blinking her eyes slowly at me.

'Cookie.'

'*Miaow*,' I answered.

'Cookie, I'm Aoi. Pleased to meet you.'

Then she gave me some water.

It felt like a dream to see the misanga in my hand!

I'd been against getting a cat. The thought of it damaging my manga was unbearable, and I saw right through the fact that it was supposed to help with my illness, which I hated. If I agreed to it, it would mean I really was ill, I thought.

But this cat, Cookie, had found Mari's misanga! She'd lost it in my room a long, long time ago.

Cookie was thirstily lapping up the water I'd put down for her.

Mari had always loved cats.

Come to think of it, the first time she ever came over to my house was because she'd wanted to see our cat, Jessica. Jessica had been with my parents since before I was born and she was old by then, so really laid-back. Mari and I wept when she died, and I remember we took her to the crematorium together.

My parents didn't seem to want to get another cat after that, so Mari and I started feeding a local stray – a huge, dirty, feral thing that came and sat by my balcony door from time to time. We fed it dry cat food outside, which it scoffed down impressively fast.

'Thank you, Cookie,' I told her.

*Miaow*, she answered.

Aoi lived in this two-storey house with her parents. Her father didn't pay much attention to me – and I didn't take any notice of him, either. Her mother had been the one who'd brought me here. She always greeted me properly, so I'd miaow back when I felt like it.

She would come home once during the day to make lunch for Aoi, before hurrying back out. Aoi would wake up around noon and eat her meal in silence. But she always fed me first, so she was my owner, and I was her cat . . . was what I thought.

Aoi stayed home all day and I often couldn't even tell whether she was alive or dead. There were lots of fun-looking things in her room, but I'd never seen her play with any of them.

Even if I invited her to play with me, she just gazed at me blankly without moving. And she never let me go outside, either.

She spent almost all the time in bed with her eyes closed, and slept as much as we cats do. Where she was different to a cat was that she often wept. Mama had told me that if you cry all the time, you get great big black bags under your eyes. Well, I told Aoi that too, but I don't know if she understood.

I didn't even know why Aoi was so sad. I sometimes cried because I missed Mama, but I wasn't sad all the time like she was.

It was depressing to see her like that.

I spent the first winter of my life mostly holding my breath inside that quiet room.

It was spring before I knew it.

I didn't sleep a wink at night during the winter. I would lie awake thinking how I'd go outside in the morning – and I really did feel like going outside at the time, but once the sun was up I was seized with anxiety just at the thought of it. What would I do if I were gripped by pain so intense it would stop my heart? What if I couldn't breathe? I would freeze just thinking about it. I was terrified.

But still, I did really want to. So I started reducing the number of things I could do at home. If there wasn't anything to do, maybe I would be able to go out. I got rid of my phone and the TV, and even threw away my books and manga.

I'd become as light as could be, but still I couldn't move.

I just kept beating myself up about everything, for hurting Mari and for hurting my parents.

I'd started eating meals on my own most of the time, too, since I didn't want anyone to see me.

Even when I felt panicky and like I was being crushed, there was nothing I could do about it.

Mari no longer appeared to me in dreams.

Even her ghost had abandoned me.

Spring came and the cherry trees blossomed. They were the most beautiful thing I'd ever seen.

Aoi's curtains had always been closed, but now she opened them, and we sat side by side gazing at the rows of blossom outside.

I felt a presence on the balcony. There was a huge, fat male cat with dirty fur on the other side of the glass.

He who strikes the first blow wins! I thought, taking up a fighting pose.

'You wanna fight me?' he asked.

'Sure. Bring it on!' I said, and gave the window a wallop. There was nothing to fear through the glass. I was absolutely safe here as long as that guy was on the other side of it, however strong he was.

'You're just as cocky as your parent, I see,' the fat cat said.

'Mama isn't cocky!' I was mightily offended by the insult.

'Your father, not your mother.'

'You knew my papa?'

'I know everything.'

'In that case, there's something I want to ask you.'

'About your father?'

'No, not about him.' I'd already heard all about Papa

from Mama. 'It's about Aoi. I'm her cat, and I want to know how she can get well again.'

'I don't know about that sort of thing.'

'And you said you knew everything! What a liar.'

'And you're a cheeky brat.' The fat cat glared at me.

Just at that moment, Aoi suddenly opened the glass door.

Aoi, what do you think you're doing?! Dumbfounded, I jumped back and hid behind the desk, scattering her things as I did so.

The fat cat grinned. Aoi put out some dry cat food on the aluminium tray. The fat cat pounced on it greedily and started to gobble it up. I watched him eat with fascination.

'You are hungry, aren't you?'

The fat cat took no notice, but continued devouring the food. Then he licked his lips in satisfaction.

'I'll ask about it. By way of thanks for the food.'

'Ask? You mean you can talk with Aoi?' I said excitedly.

'I'll ask Jon. Jon knows everything,' the fat cat said, turning his broad rear to me and leaping up on to the balcony railing with surprising agility. He turned his head and looked down. 'I'm Kuro. If you're going to live here, you should at least remember the boss's name.'

'You do put on airs.'

After seeing Kuro off, I watched Aoi gather up her scattered things. In among them were the same sorts of art materials that Reina had. Reina was always busy painting, but I'd never seen Aoi so much as pick up a brush. I'd have loved to see her paint sometime.

★

It wasn't only Kuro and the crows who came to visit. Mama's friend, the white cat called Chobi, dropped by now and then too.

'Hey, Cookie!' He was always cheerful and considerate.

'Hello, Chobi. How's Mama?'

'She's fine, but the other day she got pink paint all the way down one side of her body!'

I tried to picture it, and we both giggled.

That feral Kuro never listened to me, so I didn't like him, but I loved Chobi because he always took me seriously.

Mama said that when it came to getting married I should find myself a cat who was good at hunting, but I thought I'd be better off with a decent cat like Chobi.

It was now summer, and the first anniversary of Mari's death was approaching.

It had been a whole year since I'd killed Mari.

'I said I wasn't going!' I shouted. I hadn't raised my voice for a while, and it came out hoarse. 'I'm not going.'

Mum was stony-faced.

'I'm not going!'

'How long do you intend to keep this up?'

Her objection was reasonable. In my head I knew it, but I couldn't control my emotions.

'Shut up!'

'It's the first anniversary of Mari's death. You didn't

even go to her funeral and you haven't been to visit her grave.'

I was aware of all that. I *wanted* to go. I wanted to settle everything properly, once and for all. I wanted to apologize before the grave. But I just couldn't.

'Get out!'

I physically pushed Mum out of the room and slammed the door. Cookie froze. Mum kept talking to me through the door, but I drowned her out with wordless screams.

At last I heard her go downstairs. Her footsteps sounded exhausted.

My tears flowed on and on, unstoppable.

I heard about what was wrong with Aoi from both Kuro and Aoi herself.

'I haven't been to visit Mari's grave, and I haven't even been to her house. But I just can't bring myself to go outside,' she told me through her tears.

It wasn't because she was so comfortable in this room that she didn't go out. She *couldn't* go out. It must have been hard for her to stay in the same place all this time, however comfortable it was.

She lay on the bed crying. I tried to comfort her, but she was closed up within herself.

A loud cawing of crows ripped through the air, and Aoi flinched.

Crows flew down on to the balcony. One, two – a whole lot of them. I knew exactly why they were here – they were ready to eat Aoi if she died now.

So there was an existence in this world that was weaker than mine. I felt the beginnings of an emotion I'd never felt before stirring inside me, and made up my mind: I would save Aoi.

*Pffft!* I hissed, and threw myself at the shadows in the curtain. The noise I made as I hit the window was louder than I'd expected. But it shocked the crows too, and they flew off amid a flapping of wings.

'Cookie, are you all right?'

Got 'em! I couldn't control my excitement and ran round and round the room in circles.

And then it was autumn, and just as the trees were losing their leaves, Aoi grew more and more emaciated and quarrelled a lot with her mother. She often didn't get out of bed all day, which meant I had to find the dry food by myself.

One evening, Chobi came round at a different time than usual.

'Cookie, I've got some bad news. Mimi isn't well.'

'Mama?'

'She wants to see you.'

'But I can't get out of here.'

'I suppose not. If there's anything you'd like to say to her, I can tell her for you.'

I thought for a while, but I couldn't think of anything I could put into words.

'Tell her to do her best!'

'I will. She will be happy to hear from you.'

Aoi got up. Chobi spotted her and disappeared from the balcony in a flash.

'Aoi, I want to see Mama. She's ill, and I want to go see her.'

Aoi didn't say anything and stroked my back. The bell on the misanga around her wrist tinkled. She didn't understand what I was saying and didn't want to let me go.

I started to feel angry. I bit into the misanga and pulled as hard as I could.

'Cookie, stop that!' she yelled. 'What are you doing?'

Please, Aoi. Let me go see Mama.

'Stop it! Go away!'

She took the misanga from me and curled up in bed.

I decided to go and see Mama by myself.

At lunchtime, when Aoi's mother came home and took the laundry outside to hang it up, I slipped out past the drying area and came out on to the roof.

'I can jump from the roof too, you know!' I remembered saying to Mama.

'Yes, of course you can!'

With Mama's voice ringing in my ears, I launched myself into space.

Cookie ran away!

And it's all my fault – I told her to go away.

Cats who've lived their whole life indoors can't survive outside. When our previous cat, Jessica, managed to get out, I found her in the road in front of our house. She'd been hit by a car.

Cookie wasn't familiar with this area, so she wouldn't be able to make her way back. But my parents were both out at work. I *had* to go and rescue her.

Still, I couldn't move. I had no control over my mind and body. After missing the first anniversary of Mari's death, something in me had definitively broken and I was reduced to the most basic existence. What to do? But I couldn't do anything other than stay shivering under the duvet.

Mari! Mari, please help me!

The world without a ceiling.

Looking up at the piercingly blue sky, I was terrified that it would suck me in. I tried not to look up as I ran.

I kept on running, then suddenly realized: this world was not what I thought it was. It was much, much bigger than I'd imagined. I was scared, just like Aoi was scared of it too.

I'd thought that if I just got outside and ventured a little way, I'd soon get to Mama's place. After all, Chobi and Kuro were always dropping by.

I smelled another cat.

I panicked, and ran like hell to get away from the smell. There was nothing to protect me here.

I'd never known that the world was such a big and complicated place. I kept running through the unfamiliar streets until eventually, exhausted, I decided to take a rest under some tall plants. Big mistake.

By the time I realized I wasn't alone, it was too late. A huge female cat stood there before me.

'Get out,' she hissed, her voice cold as ice.

'Hold on a sec!'

She bared her sharp claws and came after me.

I dashed away but she caught the base of my tail. Ow, that hurt! I kept running. My rump hurt, and I had no idea where I was. Would I ever be able to find my way home . . .?

Just thinking about it made me want to weep, but I didn't. I was scared that the cat would hear and come after me.

One thought had been haunting me all this time. If only I'd gone to see Mari right away to tell her, 'I'm sorry, that was a terrible thing to say,' she would probably still be alive.

I didn't want to keep repeating the same mistake over and over.

If I went looking for Cookie, I could probably save her. I didn't want her to die. I had to rescue her! She protected me from the crows that time. Now it was my turn to save her . . .

I got out of bed and put on a coat.

Mari, give me strength. I'm begging you!

*Tinkle.* Mari's misanga gave me courage, and I moved easily through the house. There was no problem with my body – it was fine.

This time, I would be able to go out. With a confidence I hadn't had before, I opened the front door a crack.

Then my legs froze, and I could not take even a single step further.

It felt as if a vacuum outside was sucking everything out through the front door. I couldn't breathe. It was no good – there was no way I could go out.

Closing the door, I stumbled and fell over. Everything started to go dark.

Just then, I felt something tug at my wrist.

*Tinkle.*

The misanga had caught on the door handle and slid off. Reaching out for it, I slumped heavily against the door.

*Tinkle.*

With my finger, I touched Mari's misanga hanging there from the handle. Without realizing it, I had taken a step forward to remove it and had one foot beyond the front door.

All the blood in my body drained out of me. It's okay, I told myself, I have Mari's misanga. It was in my hand, broken in two. Of course! In tearing, Mari's misanga had granted my wish. Now I could go outside.

I stepped out of the front door, with both feet. This time

of my own free will. Out into the big wide world with no ceiling. Mari, thank you!

I set off confidently.

Cookie, wait for me!

The sun was going down as I dragged myself along a river-side path, and my shadow was getting disturbingly long.

It was dark and cold, and I was scared. Every time I heard the crows cawing, I panicked and cowered. I felt so helpless and powerless.

I was exhausted and hungry and more concerned about finding something to eat than trying to get home. I didn't know how to hunt down food for myself, or even where to look, so all I could do was wander around in the dark.

A delicious smell of rice and fish stock wafted past me. I made a beeline for it and glimpsed a ceramic plate piled with food. Some rice mixed with various other things and dried bonito flakes sprinkled on top. It was cooled to just the right temperature for eating.

It had probably been put there for some other cat, but I didn't care and dug straight in. I had never eaten anything so delicious in my life.

'Oi, that's my food,' a voice came from behind me, and my heart almost stopped. I gobbled up the last mouthful and nervously turned around.

Standing there was a huge, fat feral cat. I swallowed hard.

'Kuro!'

'So you remember me, Mimi's daughter.'

'My name's Cookie!'

'So have you been abandoned too?'

'No! Aoi wouldn't abandon me.'

'Then why are you here?'

'I escaped to see Mama,' I said, doing my best to put on a brave face.

'You escaped, huh?' Kuro said with a nasty laugh.

'What of it?'

'Come with me.'

He walked off and all I could do was follow.

'Were you in love with Mama too?' I asked, since Kuro wasn't talking.

'What?'

'I heard all the cats around here were in love with her.'

'Your mother's a bit full of herself, isn't she?'

'So—'

'That's enough. Just shut up and follow me.'

I felt absolutely safe with Kuro and chatted away to him, but he just remained silent.

We'd walked a long way and my legs were beginning to hurt when I started to detect familiar smells. The dry leaves, the pine resin . . . the oils Reina used to paint.

I raced on ahead of Kuro. The sun had gone down, but there was no mistaking it. It was Mama and Reina's apartment.

I took a breath and miaowed as loudly as I could. But nobody answered.

'Your mama and Reina aren't here, you know.' Kuro screwed up his face.

'You don't mean . . . Don't say that!'

A feeling of fear welled up in me. Maybe I would never see Mama again.

'Cookie!' I heard someone call.

'Aoi!' I called back.

'Cookie!'

I'd never imagined Aoi would come to get me! She was wearing a coat over her pyjamas and had slipped her bare feet into sandals. I leaped into her arms and she burst into tears.

'So you can go out again now, Aoi!' I was so happy I couldn't stop miaowing.

'Good for you,' Kuro said, and ran off. Next time he drops by our place, I thought, I'll get Aoi to give him an extra big meal.

Then I heard a car approaching. It was a taxi, and Reina got out holding a cat basket.

'Reina!'

'Cookie?!' Reina was more surprised than I'd ever seen her before.

I miaowed loudly again.

'Oh, um, I'm Cookie's—' Aoi started to explain.

'You must be her owner. She's come to see her mama, has she? Come on in,' Reina said, unlocking the apartment door.

'And Mama? How is she?' I asked Reina.

'Hold your horses! You can see her right now.'

Once we were in the apartment, Mama emerged from the cat basket wearing an awkward-looking collar around her neck. Her back leg was bandaged, and she was so much smaller than I remembered.

'My, how you've grown, Cookie!' She was weak, but her voice was steady.

'Mama, don't worry, you're going to be fine.'

'Thank you.'

I drank in Mama's smell and started grooming her fur, the way she always used to do for me. After a short while, she fell asleep.

The three of us gazed at her.

'She'll be better in no time,' Reina said.

'I'm sure she will,' Aoi replied.

# 4

THE TEMPERATURE OF THE WORLD

A summer's morning.

Kuro crouched on top of a cool breezeblock wall out of the sun, waiting. In the distance, there was the faint sound of the early-morning callisthenics played on the radio.

When it came to hunting, Kuro could wait for as long as it took.

Finally, his prey appeared – a big pile of meatballs on a plate that an elderly woman placed in front of the dog kennel. Time for the hunt!

Kuro hurled his huge body into space, turning mid-air to land on the ground on all four paws. Absorbing the shock with his body, he used the rebound to propel himself forward.

The prey was now within reach. But his rival reacted fast, too. A large figure shot out of the kennel and pounced on the plate.

If Kuro had been aiming for the plate of meatballs, he would have been beaten to it. But his goal was the bowl of water beside them. Flattening his body, he scrabbled at the surface of the water with his front paws. The water splashed up in an arc into his opponent's face, forcing him to close his eyes.

In that split second, Kuro helped himself to a meatball.

Delicious!

'Spectacular. You got me this time,' Jon said, and slowly took a meatball too.

Being praised by Jon put Kuro in a good mood. The two of them were old friends. Their friendship was mostly based on the ongoing battle of Kuro trying to get at Jon's food.

'I must be losing my touch, being outdone by you, Kuro.'

'I got strong.'

At first they really had been rivals, but now they'd come to consider themselves a good match and even felt some measure of respect for each other.

Most humans made food that was too salty, but Jon's owner knew how to bring out the flavour of the ingredients. She was now watching Kuro and Jon sitting side by side while they ate, with a smile on her face.

Once his belly was swollen with meatballs, Kuro rolled over on to his side in the shade of the dog kennel.

'You do know why animals eat food, don't you?' Jon asked dozily, pillowing his head on his front paws.

'Because they get hungry.' What a stupid question, Kuro thought.

'So why do they get hungry?'

'Because they're alive.'

'That's it,' Jon said happily and wagged his tail. 'Once

upon a time, there were some creatures that thrived without ever having to eat.'

'Not having to work for food? Sounds like paradise.'

'Paradise? I guess it was!' Jon laughed.

Then Jon told Kuro about the creatures that were driven
out of paradise.

Paradise was the place where you didn't have to work for
food, and could live happily in peace without having to
fight. There had been a brief period like that in the distant
past – although there hadn't been any humans or cats or
dogs or plants back then, just a life form shaped rather like
a leaf, which thrived so much it covered the earth. This leaf-
shaped creature was the only type of life form on earth and
gained its energy from decomposing matter in the sea, so
there wasn't any eat-or-be-eaten food chain either.

'So what did those guys spend their time doing?' Kuro eventually asked.

'They didn't do anything. They just existed. That happy
period lasted for some time.'

'So what's happened to them now?'

'They're extinct. New life forms emerged, and they were
wiped out in no time,' Jon said.

After that, the earth was filled with a mad rush of life, as
if to make up for lost time. All the different species strug-
gled to survive, fighting and eating each other. And there
were two reasons why the paradise of the leaf creatures
failed and the hell of many creatures killing each other
succeeded: diversity and competition. In the absence of

diversity, they had gone extinct for just one single reason: without competition, a superior creature better suited to the environment would not emerge.

'What *are* you going on about?' Kuro said with a big yawn.

'Simply put, paradise never lasts long.'

'In other words, it serves them right.'

'Correct.'

'You know all sorts of things, don't you, Jon?'

'We animals must know everything from when creatures originally appeared on earth up to now. Everyone else has forgotten, but I remember. That's all.'

'Right.'

Kuro liked to talk about these things with Jon. As the boss cat, he couldn't trust any of his fellow felines. But Jon wasn't interested in Kuro's territory, plus he knew a lot, which made him a perfect conversation partner.

'Kuro, have you ever wanted to know when you will die?' Jon asked out of the blue.

'Nope, not interested.' It was true. Kuro wasn't interested in anything beyond tomorrow.

'I thought you would say that,' Jon said, looking pleased.

'We can die at any time. I've often seen super-healthy guys get diarrhoea in the evening and drop dead the next morning. Lots get run over by a car and end up like an old dishrag.' It was a matter of course for Kuro that cats could die at any time. 'But then you get a cat who was so badly injured she wouldn't have been able to provide for herself, but is now up and walking around as if nothing had happened.'

'You mean Mimi? She's quite something.' Jon closed his eyes and thought for a while. Finally, as though confiding an important secret, he said, 'I don't have long left.'

Kuro was so surprised his jaw dropped, as if he'd forgotten to close his mouth.

'Jaw's come off, has it?'

'Because of your stupid joke.'

'It's not a joke.' Jon's brow furrowed.

'But that's kind of inconvenient, to say the least,' Kuro said.

'How nice of you to say so.'

'She won't be putting food out any more.'

Jon laughed.

'And you're so full of life.'

'Humans are really frightened of death . . .' Jon said, changing the subject. 'Not just of their own deaths, but of those of us dogs and cats, too.'

'Humans are weird.'

'I've seen a number of old people in this house die.'

'That's because you've lived such a long life,' Kuro said. He paused before asking, 'So have you started to fear death?'

'I don't fear death. It's no different from sleeping – it's like we practise dying every night.' Then he said hesitantly, 'It's just that I'm worried about *her*.'

'Her?'

Jon glanced up at the woman folding laundry in the room overlooking the garden. She was his owner. Her bearing was steady, but her white hairs were evident.

'She's called Shino,' Jon introduced her. The woman smiled and stood up.

'Is she your girlfriend?'

'Ha ha ha! Unfortunately, she has a husband. Although they don't live together any more.'

Kuro slowly retreated to a safe distance as Shino came over to take the empty plate away.

'Sounds like trouble. Doesn't she work?'

'She used to. She always wore a smart suit and looked really good, but she left her job.'

'Huh.' Unlike Jon, Kuro wasn't interested in the lives of humans. 'So she lives alone in this big house?'

'Yes. She used to live with a bedridden old lady who she looked after.'

'Why bother looking after old people?'

'If you don't look after them, they die.'

'I don't understand the point of looking after guys who can't survive on their own,' Kuro said, and gave a big stretch.

'Shino gave up her own life to care for that old woman as she was slowly dying.'

Kuro thought he finally understood what Jon was getting at. 'You do beat around the bush, Jon. In other words, you don't want to end up like that old bedridden woman.'

'Right.'

The conversation now over, Jon closed his eyes and went to sleep. Kuro curled up in a ball beside him.

*The bath is ready.*

After a short melody, the electronic voice announced that the bath was now full of hot water.

'Okay, coming,' Shino answered the machine, and got up from the sofa where she'd been watching TV. Having adapted the house for an invalid, there were no stairs into the bathroom, and the bathroom itself was lined with hand-rails. She herself didn't have a need for them yet, but she felt reassured they were there for whenever she did.

She kept the lights off in the bathroom as she sank slowly into the tub, a habit formed as a result of her husband's mother, who had always been admonishing her for wasting electricity. Thinking back, it had probably been a defensive reaction to this intruder in her home. After years of counter-ing it with more stubbornness, she'd grown accustomed to bathing in the dark. In hindsight, these little ways in which her mother-in-law had bullied her were nothing compared to what came later, once she became incapacitated and required nursing care.

Shino let out a deep sigh.

The rays of the moon shone down through the skylight. She scooped up some water and gazed at it cupped in her hands. It made her smile. It was because she took pleasure in things like this that she could live so cheaply.

She got out of the bath and put on her nightgown, then went up to the roof to enjoy the lukewarm breeze in the cool of evening.

A shooting star flashed in the distance and she thought of making a wish, but realized there was nothing left to hope for.

There was a beautiful moon that night. As the evening deepened, the chatter of young voices and the hum of traffic from the streets fell quiet.

By the time Kuro arrived at Jon and Shino's house, a large number of cats were already gathered in the garden – including Chobi, he noted. Any cat in town who was free was there. Noticing the boss's arrival, the cats respectfully made way for him and he trotted over to his position before Jon's kennel.

Finally, Jon came lumbering out of the kennel and looked slowly around at the gathered cats.

'It won't be long now. I will be gone tonight,' Jon informed them.

A barely audible murmur ran through the cats and, with a small nod of his head, Kuro gave the signal.

'I'll miss you, Jon,' Chobi said quietly.

Others followed with their parting words. For them, Jon was a walking encyclopaedia, as well as someone they could turn to for advice. There were fewer fights over territories, thanks to him. Jon listened in silence to their farewells, his eyes glistening.

Lastly, Kuro, as the representative of the area's cats, thanked him on behalf of all the others who weren't able to come. 'I'm sure they are all thinking about you while tucked up in their beds. Thank you, Jon.'

'Thank you, everyone,' Jon said, his voice wavering. He

deftly removed his collar with his front paws, sliding his big head out.

'You're pretty handy with that, aren't you, Jon?' Chobi said.

'It already broke some time ago.'

Lying on the dry grass, the well-worn leather collar shone like amber.

Jon shook his whole body from head to tail, and took a firm step into the moonlight.

'Jon, I really can't believe you're going to die,' Chobi said, trotting after him.

'I'm not going to die. I'm going to become eternity.'

'Eternity?' Kuro and Chobi both looked doubtful.

'If I die here, then both of you, and Shino, would know that I was dead. But if you don't see me die, then nobody will know for sure whether I'm dead or not.'

'Is that what eternity is?'

'Yup.'

Jon turned back to look at the house. There was just one room with a light on.

'Leave Shino to me,' Kuro said, puffing his chest out.

'I will, Kuro.'

It was time to go. Jon and the cats made their way together along the deserted streets.

The heat of the day lingered in the darkness, and the damp breeze coiled around them. For cats, this was a pleasant feeling. Kuro remembered something Jon had once told him: their ancestors had originally lived in a tropical country. That's why, on nights like this, they felt an inexpressible nostalgia.

The cats began to break away one by one, and returned to their own territories. Kuro and Chobi were the last to remain.

Jon stopped. 'Since you've kept me company until the end, I will give you some good news.'

'Good news?' Chobi asked.

'Some day, I will come back.'

'Come back?'

'Yes. I will probably have a different appearance, but I'm sure both of you will know it is me.'

Chobi listened, wide-eyed.

'And when I come back, I will grant your wishes, Kuro and Chobi,' Jon said in a low voice.

'Can you really do that?' Kuro looked doubtful.

'Well, in that case, I wish—' Chobi started, but Jon interrupted him.

'There's no need to say it out loud. Just wish for it in your heart.'

Chobi sat beneath the starry sky, and obediently closed his eyes.

How silly, Kuro thought. Yet still, he couldn't help but wonder, what if . . . and Shino's face rose up in the back of his mind. He wished that Shino could live a happy life. She was going to be so sad about losing Jon, so this was the least he could wish for.

Jon looked from Kuro to Chobi. 'Don't forget what you wish for. If you hold it in your heart, it will some day be granted, even if I'm not here.'

Kuro caught Chobi's eye and winked. So he was making fun of them, after all.

Jon wagged his tail.

'Now go!' Kuro said.

Jon set off at a run with more strength and speed than you would have thought an old dog capable of. Eventually, they heard him bark in the distance beyond the edge of town.

'He's a sprightly old man, isn't he? Hardly on his death-bed,' Kuro said under his breath.

'Hey, Kuro,' Chobi said on their way back.

'What?'

'What did you wish for?'

'Nothing.' That was a lie.

'Really?'

'You didn't really believe his little joke, did you?'

'It wasn't a joke. His face had the expression he always has when he says something important.'

'Maybe you're right . . .'

'I wished my girlfriend could be happy . . .' Chobi volunteered without being asked.

'You shouldn't say it out loud.' The guy was embarrassing, but, on the other hand, Kuro was rather envious of the way he was able to talk openly about that sort of thing.

'Okay, see you soon, Kuro.'

Tail in the air, Chobi ran off into the night streets, no doubt heading home to his girlfriend.

Kuro watched him go, and was lost in thought for a while. Perhaps he really should take care of Shino. He'd only said it in the heat of the moment, but now he had to take responsibility for it.

With the moon shining down on him, Kuro padded back

the way he'd come and crawled into Jon's kennel to wait for morning.

Kuro dreamed of Jon, enveloped in his smell.

Shino had a dream that was so schoolgirlish it even made her laugh.

She was riding a shooting star – a real star-shaped one – through the night sky. She was dressed in the same clothes as she wore now, but had returned to her younger self. Her body was surprisingly light.

Someone came along riding another shooting star. It was Jon. He was wearing a round glass-fronted helmet, like an astronaut.

'Hey, Jon!' she called out to him.

'Oh, hello, Shino,' Jon replied. This didn't seem at all out of place in the dream. 'Please make a wish. That's what shooting stars are for.' He winked at her.

'Well, then, I wish I was young again.'

'Aren't you already young enough?'

'Oh, I suppose I am!'

'So make another wish.'

Shino said the first thing that occurred to her. 'In that case, please make breakfast for me. Wouldn't it be lovely to wake up and find breakfast already made!'

'Leave it to me!' Jon said, tapping his chest with his front paw.

And then she woke up.

She had an uneasy premonition, maybe because she'd had such a strange dream. I don't suppose . . . she thought, but of course there was no breakfast ready and waiting for her. 'Of course there isn't!' She was amused that she had even expected it for a moment, and had to laugh.

She decided to use up yesterday's leftovers to make breakfast for herself and Jon.

Having slept soundly until morning after the late night, Kuro woke up to a delicious smell of food.

He dragged himself out of the kennel and looked up to see Shino standing there, gazing down at him.

'Oh my,' she said, her eyes round with surprise.

'Shino, this is hard to say, but . . . last night, Jon went on a journey.' Kuro did his best to explain in his own way. Of course she couldn't understand, but she noticed Jon's collar lying on the ground and seemed to get the general idea.

'Since I made this, how about you eat it?'

Kuro had Jon's breakfast all to himself. When he was young, he had always thought that one day he would eat up all of Jon's breakfast, but somehow getting it without having to compete for it made it seem tasteless.

'Would you like to be my cat?'

Even though she'd gone to the trouble of inviting him to

live with her, his pride made him turn her down. 'I'm a feral cat, I don't belong to anyone.'

Having polished off the breakfast, Kuro left Shino's house. He had lots of work to do as the boss.

The next morning, Kuro decided to go and check on Shino again. I'm too nice to people, he thought, but Jon had entrusted her to him, so he didn't have much choice.

She had already prepared breakfast for him, even though he hadn't asked for it. He decided to accept it gratefully. It was as delicious as always. The balance of fish broth and chicken was just to his taste.

He gobbled it down contentedly, and suddenly, looking up, caught sight of Shino watching him.

If she made fresh meals for him every day, he couldn't very well let them go to waste, could he? He'd better come and check on her daily from now on.

In the end, it was too much bother to keep coming and going, so he decided to make a habit of sleeping in Jon's kennel. Shino often tried to get him to come into the house, but Kuro refused. If he went into the house, he would no longer be a feral cat. Even if she did feed him, his sleeping place was outside in Jon's kennel.

Kuro and Shino took to sitting together for chats on the veranda of the old house. Both of them needed someone to talk to after Jon had gone.

Shino gently stroked Kuro's back. Kuro had never let a human touch his fur before. The first time he'd nearly jumped out of his skin, but he put up with it, and while she stroked him he began to realize that it actually felt surprisingly good.

Shino lived alone in the old house. All she talked of were people who were either dead or no longer living here.

It happened at a time when I was young and beautiful, and still full of life.

My husband's father, my father-in-law, collapsed with a blood clot in the brain and needed nursing.

Mindful about what people would say, my mother in law insisted on nursing him at home, and my husband agreed with her. None of us realized just how hard that would be, and since we spent a lot of money on adapting the house to accommodate his disabilities, there was no going back later.

Nursing someone at home is a burden on both the carer and the cared for.

My father-in-law was proud, having occupied a high position overseeing others at his company, and he never could accept his situation right until the end. Having once been so distinguished, he began to lose his temper at the slightest provocation. Whenever he called, we had to go to him right away; he always found fault with the way we served or cleared away his meals; he got angry, threatened us, and grew violent. He became a slave to paranoia.

My mother-in-law put up with a lot, and I ended up resigning from my sales job at a pharmaceutical company in order to help her. My boss at the time tried to stop me and recommended using a nursing home, but my husband wouldn't hear of it. On my last day at work, my boss told me, 'It's your life, and you have to make sure you keep enough of it for yourself.' It was only much later that I understood what he meant.

We had to nurse my father-in-law for longer than we'd expected. When he did eventually die, my mother-in-law put her hands together and said, 'Thank you.'

Soon after, she started showing symptoms of dementia. By that time, my husband was barely ever at home, so I had to look after her alone. Her behaviour became every bit as bad as my father-in-law's had been. She'd hated the tyranny he had wielded over her, but now she did the same to me. I had to deal with the stress alone, but even so, I couldn't neglect her and continued to nurse her.

I was now too old to go back to work, and I had my pride hurt with regards to my husband, who spent all his time with another woman.

By the end, my mother-in-law would shout and grow violent at the slightest little thing, and she died not even knowing who she was.

All that was left was this house, adapted for invalids, and myself, now utterly exhausted.

My husband and I never did have children. Things might have been different if we had. He worked in social services and travelled all around the country giving talks on geriatric nursing and treatment, without knowing anything of the frontline of nursing care happening in his own home.

'My husband left . . . and now I'm all alone in this empty house.' Shino gave a lonely laugh.

'Hmm.' Kuro knew nothing of this kind of world.

'I sometimes wonder what my life is all about, you know . . .' she said, and tickled Kuro under his chin. 'You're so lucky, being free.'

Kuro had lived his whole life being free, so he well knew that freedom came at a price. 'You have somewhere to sleep, heating, and food. Doesn't sound so bad to me.'

Shino narrowed her eyes in a smile. 'Jon has gone, but . . . I'm glad that you came along.' She looked happy.

Oi. This woman needs toughening up. Kuro stood up and straightened his tail. 'Come with me.'

He decided to take Shino for a walk. How cats live is something you learn on the streets. Shino was getting on in years, but it wasn't too late for her to start something new.

He patiently taught her about the lives of cats, much as he would have taught a kitten who didn't have any manners.

First of all, you had to secure drinking water. There was water you could drink, and water you couldn't. The water in puddles was dirty and would upset your stomach. The water in park fountains at first glance looked clean, but since they were just sending the same water round and round, it also upset your stomach. The water in drinking fountains was safe. Licking the drips from taps quenched your thirst.

Next, he decided to teach her about hunting. If you could catch prey, you could live anywhere. It was also exhilarating and fun. You needed to add a bit of tension to life.

'Wait here, Shino.'

Kuro jumped into the long grass in front of her, snatched a grasshopper and took it back to her. This was the level of prey it would be best to start with, he thought.

He dropped the grasshopper at her feet.

'My, you are clever, aren't you?'

He'd gone to all the trouble of catching it for her, and she'd let it get away! 'Foolish woman! Do you want to learn or not?'

However much he scolded her, though, she just said things like, 'How clever you are!' and stroked his back, so after a while, he couldn't be bothered any more.

Oh well. She could learn it little by little.

One day Shino and Kuro were out on their now regular morning walk when they spotted a woman whose smell he recognized from somewhere.

'Good morning, Aoi,' Shino said.

'Oh, good morning!'

It was Cookie's owner, the woman who had come to collect Cookie when she'd got lost. She looked a lot neater than last time he'd seen her. Her colour was good, and she was now quite beautiful.

'Are you on your way to work?'

'Yes, I'm starting today.'

'Oh, how wonderful. Do your best!'

'I will. That cat . . . is he yours? He looks just like a cat that sometimes comes to our place.'

'In that case, it's probably him. He now has free room and board at my place.'

'Free room and board, huh? Lucky boy!' Aoi said, crouching down before Kuro and showing him the palm of her hand.

Kuro sniffed her despite himself. But it was a trap. Aoi grabbed him and, turning him over, stroked his belly. Kuro twisted his body to get away, but it felt so good that eventually he stopped protesting.

She was clearly used to handling cats . . .

'How's Cookie?' he asked, but of course for Aoi it just sounded like he was miaowing.

'I've got a cat too. She's still a kitten, though . . . She recently managed to get out of the house and went to see her mother.'

'That was smart of her.'

'No, no, I had to show her the way!' Kuro protested, but of course the humans didn't understand him. Not that it really mattered.

Kuro and Shino said goodbye to Aoi and decided to make their way home. Kuro wanted to look around his territory a bit more, but Shino already seemed tired.

When they reached home, he felt a presence in the garden.

'I don't suppose . . . Is it Jon? Has he come back?'

Kuro broke into a run and peered into the kennel, but Jon wasn't there.

Somebody was sleeping on the veranda. It wasn't Jon, but a young man. He was wearing a worn-out suit and had with him a plastic bag from a convenience store, and his face was pale.

Kuro didn't know who he was, but he didn't sense any danger from him. He smelled very similar to Shino.

'Ryota, is that you?' Shino asked.

The man opened his eyes, but didn't move. He looked like he'd collapsed from exhaustion. 'Hello, Auntie, long time no see.' He smiled.

'It sure is. What's up?'

'Auntie, I'm begging you, if anyone calls, please don't tell them I'm here. And whatever you do, don't tell Dad,' Ryota pleaded. He sounded really desperate.

'You're in a bind, are you? Okay, come on in,' Shino said, ushering her unexpected guest inside.

It's not like I had any particular ambition or was aiming too high. I just wanted to live a normal life.

I didn't have any particular talent, but then I didn't have any particular burden to bear either. My grades weren't all that good, but not so bad that I had to worry about failing. I hadn't done anything particularly praiseworthy to earn public recognition, but then I hadn't done anything so bad that my parents would have to punish me.

I'd often been chosen to compete in track and field events in high school, but I hadn't broken any records at the prefectural sports competitions. I'd never been hospitalized for any illness or injury, and there had never been anything like my parents divorcing or being in terrible debt, or any friends that had committed suicide or anything.

I lived a normal life, taking exams like everyone else around me. I went to a local university and spent my days doing my own thing. But then when it came to finding a job, I couldn't find one anywhere. For the first time, it somehow dawned on me that this society didn't need me.

I had no idea what was wrong with me. I'd just been living my life like everyone else around me. It was like the ladder I'd been climbing had been pulled away and I'd been left hanging there in space. What I'd thought was normal life turned out to be possible only for smart guys or those with special talents.

Maybe I'd been wrong to assume that if I just did the same as everyone else, I'd be able to get by. People said all sorts of things, like it was to do with my generation, or the state of the economy, or that young people couldn't pick and choose jobs. It might have felt good to say that the world was wrong, but that didn't solve the problem.

I was in a bind, but then in the autumn my parents found a job for me. It was one of those aimed at new graduates who had failed in the standard April employment intake. I was surprised since I didn't think my parents had any connections, but I gratefully grabbed the opportunity.

It was in an IT company. I didn't have any experience of computers or programming, but I was willing to do anything. However, the training for new employees consisted not of programming or how to use computers, but of digging a big hole for no reason. All of us newbies worked together to dig a hole that was deeper than we were tall. All the while, they yelled at us as we kept digging. We kept digging until blisters formed on our hands and burst, until finally the hole was made.

Our supervisor praised us for a job well done, but we were so exhausted that we were in tears. I had a feeling of achievement I'd never experienced before. I thought I'd finally been accepted by this company. Thinking back now, that was just an old ruse of theirs.

After that, I threw myself into my work. The project I was assigned to after minimal training was doomed to fail from the start, and I worked hard and felt more exhausted than I had when digging the hole.

Spirit was more important than ability in this company and you could get by if your voice was loud enough, even if you didn't have any skills.

I had to stay in a hotel near the client's office without going home for several months. One day, when I didn't even have a free moment to go back to the hotel, I was in the office kitchenette about to make some of the cup noodles kept for employees, as usual, when I realized I no longer knew how to prepare them.

I still don't quite understand what happened, but I had no idea in which order to open all the little packets of soup and condiments, or how to put them in the cup. However many times I read the instructions, I just couldn't understand them.

Suddenly, I felt like I was having a breakdown, and a chill ran down my back. I left the half-made cup noodles in the darkened kitchenette and walked out via the emergency stairs so as not to be seen by anyone.

My watch read six o'clock, but my surroundings looked awfully yellow. Maybe I'd been staring at the computer screen for too long. There was hardly anyone around in the business district, and I felt as though I'd got lost in another world.

I reached the station and finally realized that it wasn't six in the evening, but six in the morning. I got on the first train I saw, sat in an empty seat, and fell asleep. I'd left my phone somewhere. I'd probably thrown it away without noticing.

When a crowd of people started to board the train at a station, I woke up. It occurred to me that if I changed there, I could go to my aunt's place. I hadn't seen her for years, but she'd always been fond of me. I just wanted to see her. She at least would accept me.

Ryota slept through breakfast and lunch. He was just like a cat, Kuro thought.

'He's my nephew,' Shino told him. He was her elder brother Tasuke's son, apparently.

From that day on, Shino cooked for two (as well as for Kuro). Whenever Ryota suggested he should leave, she told him to stay longer.

'Dad used his connections to get me into that job, so he'll lose face through this. No way can I go home now.'

'You can stay here as long as you like.'

Little by little, Ryota began to talk about what had happened to him. His story was beyond Kuro's imagination, but still he understood that Ryota had escaped from some terrible place. Shino was indignant about how awful some companies were.

Slowly, Ryota recovered. Shino was pleased, but Kuro thought he was becoming a nuisance. Now the guy was getting better, it just meant there was one more person he had to look out for. When Ryota rudely dangled a string in front of him, Kuro grabbed it, paws outstretched, and mercilessly showed him who was boss.

At heart, Shino probably liked looking after people. Kuro had the feeling that she had more energy than before.

Over the summer, Ryota became well enough to go out for walks and help with the housework.

'You're lucky to be free,' Ryota said with a smile, watching Kuro as he ate.

'You humans are freer than we cats, though.' Humans could eat whatever they wanted and go wherever they pleased.

Whenever Ryota tried to tease him, Kuro would lash out with a paw, but Ryota never learned. As always, he grabbed Kuro and tried to stroke him – and, as always, Kuro wriggled out of his grasp.

During one of these moments, Kuro noticed Chobi sauntering over to them.

'But it feels nice when people stroke you!' Chobi told him.

'By all means, be my guest,' Kuro retorted, knowing full well that Chobi never let anyone other than his owner stroke him.

'How earnest Ryota is,' Chobi said.

That day Shino had asked Ryota to do some work in the garden, and there were piles of weeds he'd removed lying around the place.

'Even clumsy idiots have good points.'

Kuro and Chobi sat side by side watching him work.

'People who are too earnest can't bring themselves to blame others, so they end up blaming themselves and suffering for it.'

Chobi was spineless for a cat, but he knew a lot about people, Kuro thought. 'That must be tough,' he said, then realized something. 'Your owner's the same, isn't she?'

'Yeah, they're really similar,' Chobi said, looking a bit desolate.

Shino discovered to her surprise that she enjoyed teaching Ryota. She'd never had the opportunity to teach anyone before, and nobody had ever asked her. Even if it was only household chores, watching Ryota grow was fun.

It might have been like this if she'd had a son, she thought. Somehow this made daily life feel fuller.

To begin with, Ryota hadn't had a clue about housework, and Shino had thrown herself into teaching him how to do everything, from cooking rice to polishing the glass doors. And she'd found him to be a receptive pupil worthy of her efforts.

After three months, they were at ease with each other and able to chat comfortably. Shino had long forgotten what a pleasure it was to sit with someone at the dinner table and chat casually about the day.

★

And then came the day she'd feared.

The doorbell rang early in the morning. Someone was aggressively pressing the button over and over again.

'Ryota! I know you're in there!' It was Shino's brother Tasuke's voice.

'It's my father . . .' Ryota stopped in the middle of preparing breakfast, and turned white as a sheet.

'Don't worry,' Shino told him.

She took a deep breath and turned off the stove. Kuro, who now usually came into the kitchen to wait for breakfast, slowly got up. Shino exchanged a look with him. She had the feeling he was telling her, Hup. Let's do it!

It was time to go into battle.

She could see several figures through the glass of the front door. Grown men coming en masse to threaten an old lady. Whatever next!

For the first time in many years, a hot feeling welled up within the depths of Shino's body. It was an emotion she hadn't felt even when her husband left. She was angry. Kuro's hackles were raised, as if he'd been infected by her rage. That's right, Kuro. We have to fight to protect our territory.

'Ryota! Come out here!' Tasuke banged angrily on the door.

Undaunted by the noise he was making, Shino opened the door. Tasuke stood there with the black-suited men he'd brought with him.

'Hello, Tasuke. It has been a long time, hasn't it?' she said quietly, her voice calm.

'Where's Ryota?'

'Please leave.'

Tasuke's expression changed. 'Shut up and get my son out here.'

'You still haven't learned any manners, have you?'

'Dad, stop this,' Ryota said, coming out.

He'll ruin everything by coming out here now, Shino thought.

Seeing his son there before him after so long, Tasuke warmed to his theme. 'Ryota, you've really rubbed my face in it, haven't you.'

Ryota had come out assertively, but now quailed before his father.

'Which is more important, Tasuke, your honour or your son's life?' Shino asked calmly.

'Oh, you do exaggerate!' Tasuke didn't even bother hiding his irritation.

'Exaggerate? How?' Shino took a deep breath and looked her brother in the eye. 'Please leave now.'

Discomfort showed in Tasuke's eyes. It had been a long time since his sister had left the family home, and she was no longer the weak, indecisive little girl he'd known.

One of the men he'd brought with him caught hold of Shino's arm.

*Ssshyaaaaaaaassszl* A voice that seemed to reverberate from deep in the earth ripped through the air as Kuro threatened him – a wild growl that sounded like it was cutting through cloth, ready for battle.

Tasuke and the black suits took an involuntary step back.

'How amusing,' Shino said, shaking free of the man's hand. 'A group of grown men frightened of a cat. Whatever next!'

Tasuke was clearly flustered. 'What do you intend to do with my son?'

'Me? Nothing. Just wait.'

They glared at each other. Tasuke looked away first.

'I'll be back.'

'Next time I'll call the police,' she said to his departing back.

'Auntie . . . thank you . . .' Ryota said after Tasuke and the other men had gone. He sounded on the verge of tears, and Kuro smacked him on the leg a few times, as if telling him to pull himself together.

'So, let's have breakfast,' Shino said as brightly as she could. Then she slowly relaxed her hands. She had been clenching her fists so hard that they'd gone white.


The season turned into winter.

Kuro woke up earlier than usual, and stepped on Shino's belly on his way to his litter tray.

'Oooof,' Shino groaned in her sleep.

The dim light just before dawn was an ideal time to go out hunting, but he didn't feel like leaving the house in this freezing weather.

It was cold in the bathroom where his litter tray was, but it was definitely much better than outside, he thought, then shook his head. This wouldn't do! That way of thinking was for pet cats. Sleeping in blankets! Well, maybe just for the winter . . .

Kuro was staying with Shino over the cold winter months, and having two freeloaders in the house was keeping her busy.

She'd wanted to give him a bath, and at first he'd run around to get away from her, but she'd ended up sneakily grabbing him when he was fast asleep and dumping him in the tub. Once he'd got used to it, though, the custom of soaking in warm water felt good. What a waste to let humans keep it to themselves.

He finished his business and kicked at the white cat litter with his back feet. This toilet thing was pretty comfortable, too.

A light was on in the kitchen. It was Ryota's role to make breakfast now. At first he'd been a terrible cook and had made everything too salty, but now, well, it wasn't too bad. Shino kept saying how delightful it was to have been liberated from getting up early.

Kuro was just about to go back to bed when he sensed a long-missed presence. And this presence, he remembered, did actually have a name.

'Jon!'

As the beloved name came from his mouth, he sensed with some regret that it had been quite a while since he'd last thought of his old friend.

'Jon!!!' he cried, louder this time.

He squeezed through the cat flap and ran around outside, not even flinching at the piercingly cold winter morning. The clouds hung low in the sky, and white flakes were falling.

Snow.

Come to think of it, Jon had loved snow.

'Jon! Are you there?' Kuro sped around the garden, calling for his friend.

'What's up, Kuro? It's cold out here!' Ryota came out of the kitchen bundled up in warm clothes.

'Ryota, look!' Kuro raised his head to the sky.

'Oh, it's snowing!' Ryota looked up too.

'He's bound to come back on a day like this!' Kuro said, and dashed off.

'Hey, where are you going? You haven't had your breakfast yet!'

Kuro ran as fast as he could through the crisp morning air. The snow was falling in thick flakes now.

'Kuro, wait, won't you?'

He heard loud clattering footsteps behind him and realized that Ryota was following him. 'Come on, Ryota! You might get your wish granted!'

Kuro kept running and running, not caring whose territory he was in. He ran up the slope and jumped from the guard rail to the fence, then from there to the automatic vending machine, before kicking off from there to another wall. Always up, going ever higher. Nothing else mattered, not territories or anything else.

He had the feeling Jon was calling him. A strong wind was bringing more snow now, but still he kept running, kicking the asphalt with all four paws.

'Jon!' he heard another cat call. It was Chobi coming up the slope after him.

'Chobi!'

The two of them ran side by side.

The first morning train was departing the station, and they heard the loud noise of it moving over the elevated tracks. Energized by the sound, they ran on together. They were aiming for the top of the slope.

The wooden apartment building where Mimi lived came into view. There was a light on in her apartment. Reina had probably been up all night painting.

They ran on, chasing the snow. The slope started to dip downwards as they cut through the shrine and along a street of new-build houses. Onwards, onwards!

They passed by Cookie and Aoi's house. It had a new mailbox with a picture of a marble-patterned cat that looked like Cookie.

'A picture of Cookie!' Chobi shouted. Kuro could see that without being told.

Kuro and Chobi kept on running. Jon's presence was getting closer. They reached a small hill, and a steep staircase came into view.

'Don't tell me you're climbing up there,' they heard Ryota gasp pitifully behind them.

'Jon!' Kuro shouted.

'He's just up there!' Chobi also sensed him.

At last, they reached the highest point in the town. On top of the hill was a little park with a small bench.

The snowflakes were even bigger now, and falling more thickly. They could see the train passing by

'Looks like the snow's going to settle . . .'

'Yeah, it does.'

Chobi and Kuro sat watching the train for a while. The town, just waking from sleep, its heartbeat starting up, was sprawled out below them.

Ryota finally caught up with them, trying to get his breath back. 'Kuro . . . what on earth are you doing?' he said, gasping for air. He was such a weakling for someone so young.

Chobi looked around. He could hear a woman's footsteps coming from the other direction.

'Chobi!'

A woman with short hair and wearing a big overcoat appeared. Her bulky appearance made her look like a large cat, Kuro thought.

'My girlfriend,' Chobi said proudly.

She looked taken aback to see Ryota. She probably hadn't expected to find anyone else up there.

'Oh, that's my cat,' Ryota said, also flustered by her arrival.

'Shino's my owner, not you. I'm *her* cat,' Kuro said, disgruntled, but Ryota wasn't listening. He couldn't take his eyes off Chobi's owner.

She reached her arms out to Chobi, who jumped into them with a practised air. 'I was so surprised when he ran off like that.'

'Yeah, our Kuro did the same . . . ha ha ha.' Ryota laughed goofily.

The two looked at each other.

'It's the first snow of winter, isn't it?' she said, finally.

'So it is,' Ryota answered.

★

Jon's presence had vanished, Kuro suddenly realized, and he began to shiver.

'Kuro, it looks like my wish has been granted.'

'What?'

Chobi was looking up at his girlfriend's face. She was glowing, Kuro noticed. Somehow the look on her face reminded him of Shino lately. Then he finally understood: his wish had long been granted too, hadn't it?

He also realized something else: he would never see Jon again.

'Thank you, my friend,' he murmured to the sky beyond the snow clouds.

EPILOGUE

The long, long winter came to an end, and the cherry blossom season arrived.

I was walking along the river under the blossoms with Chobi in a pet-carrier. The pale pink petals billowed in the air like smoke.

The fluttering revealed air currents invisible to the eye.

'It's not your fault – you can't see what people are feeling,' the person beside me had once told me.

This had made me feel better about myself. Until then, I'd blamed myself for not understanding how people felt. I couldn't see what everyone else could see, and because of that, I hurt the people around me.

I didn't even really understand my own feelings, either. I'd been overthinking things under the illusion that I'd actually understood how people felt and was only pretending that I hadn't.

Someone had taught me this, and I'd met that someone thanks to Chobi.

Blossoms drifted down on the breeze.

'It's pretty, isn't it, Chobi?'

Chobi responded with a *miaow*.

After we met in the park that snowy morning, we met up from time to time and talked. It was better to get to know each other slowly, I thought.

I recalled that rainy day when I'd rescued Chobi – or so I'd arrogantly believed at the time. Actually, I was the one who'd been rescued.

'Oi, Mimi, come on down from there!' Masato called.

Mimi was on top of the bookcase, threatening him. Her injured leg had healed, and she was now able to run around at will.

'Stop messing around and help me with the packing,' I told him, as I wrapped up some dishes in newspaper.

'Oi, Reina. Remember who's the senior one here . . .' Masato retorted. Still, he conscientiously started tying up some bundles of magazines with string.

I'd somehow managed to pass the exam and had been admitted to the same art university as Masato, although I was one year below him.

I'd decided to live with my parents and commute from there, so I was leaving this apartment.

'Hey, you read manga like this? That's a surprise!' Masato said, tying up a pile of monthly manga magazines.

'Only because a friend of mine has a manga in it.'

'Wow, you have a friend who's a professional manga artist?'

It was Cookie's owner, Aoi. She was back at work now, and had also recently started serializing a four-frame manga about a cat. Ever since she and Cookie had come over to see Mimi, we'd been good friends. They still came to visit sometimes. Cookie was over a year old now and quite the independent young lady.

A cherry blossom petal floated in on the breeze through the wide-open window, and I suddenly started to feel sentimental.

I too was now stepping out into a whole new world.

We were in her apartment, sitting side by side and gazing at the deep ultramarine sky. The wind howled as wisps of clouds raced by.

I felt her slim fingers touching my fur.

'Hey, Chobi,' she said.

'What is it?' I answered.

She didn't say anything, but I knew what she was thinking. I felt the same way as she did.

I love this world. This thought came to me with absolute clarity.

Suddenly she laughed, and I looked up at her happy, glowing face. She'd picked up on my thoughts, too.

I'm sure that she, too, loves this world.

Makoto Shinkai is the hugely popular anime filmmaker of *Your Name*. His debut novel, *She and Her Cat*, was a bestseller in Japan. It is inspired by his highly praised five-minute anime in which he highlights the gentle magic of the everyday alongside the importance of communication and connection. It will be published in fourteen languages around the world.

Ginny Tapley Takemori is the award-winning translator of *Convenience Store Woman*, *Earthlings* and *Life Ceremony* by Sayaka Murata, and the co-translator of *The Little House* by Kyōko Nakajima, amongst other acclaimed Japanese fiction. She lives in rural Japan.